ONCE UPON A WHILE

revised

a third memoir by forrest fenn

Published by

ONE HORSE LAND & CATTLE CO.

P.O. Box 8174

Santa Fe, New Mexico 87504

Second printing

ISBN: 978-0-692-19628-1

Sketches by Forrest Fenn

Treasure photograph (Foreword) by Addison Doty

Photograph of Forrest (Foreword) by Sven Doornkaat

ONCE UPON A WHILE

revised
a third memoir by forrest fenn

To all of my experiences both good and bad.
You taught me so much.

TREASURE OF ANOTHER KIND
foreword by douglas preston

I first met Forrest Fenn in the Dragon Room of the Pink Adobe in the late 1980s, where he habitually occupied a table in the corner, which featured a rotating cast of eclectic Santa Feans, including John Ehrlichman, Larry Hagman, Clifford Irving, Ali MacGraw, and Rosalea Murphy. I joined the table as a young, unknown, and struggling writer, wondering how the mistake had been made inviting me among all these famous people. But Forrest Fenn was an outstanding lunch companion, telling story after story that kept the table enthralled, and we instantly hit it off. That was the beginning of my friendship with Forrest, who is one of the most remarkable people I have ever met. Here is a man who came from a small town in Texas, barely graduated from high school, spent 20 years in the Air Force as a fighter pilot, flew 328 combat missions in Vietnam over a period of 348 days, survived being shot down twice, and was awarded a raft of medals; he then retired, moved to Santa Fe, and built a world-famous gallery that put Santa Fe on the art-world map; he ran the gallery for 18 years with his wife Peggy and together they raised a wonderful family. Along the way he also published 10 books (this is the 11th), acquired and partially excavated a 5,000 room prehistoric Indian pueblo, and amassed a peerless collection of Native American antiquities and art.

I knew I was a friend of Forrest's when, in the early 1990s, he invited me into his vault. This walk-in fortified room, hidden in the back of a closet, was filled with extraordinary treasures — Pre-Columbian gold artifacts, Indian peace medals, a Ghost Dance shirt, the greatest collection of Clovis points in existence, and (later) Sitting Bull's celebrated peace pipe. Forrest had been a dealer in art and antiquities for years, with many superb objects passing through his hands. These were the things he had kept, the best of the best. Forrest liked artifacts that told stories, and each one had a rich and fabulous history.

In that first visit to the vault, Forrest wanted to show me something quite specific. He explained that he had been diagnosed with cancer. Although it was in remission, the prognosis was not good. He did not, he said, wish to linger in weakness and pain, and he especially did not want to put his family through a long and difficult ordeal as he wasted away from cancer. The honorable and dignified solution for all concerned, he told me, was to end it quickly and cleanly, by suicide.

But Forrest is a complicated human being, and with him nothing is simple. He had worked out a plan to end his life that would, he hoped, give something back to the world and encourage people to explore the outdoors he loved, while at the same time generating high interest, if not consternation. Forrest was never one to shy away from causing a stir.

On the right side of the vault, on a sturdy shelf, sat a bronze casket of ancient workmanship that he had recently acquired. Gene Thaw, the noted collector, had identified it as a rare Romanesque lock-box dating back to 1150 A.D. He opened the lid to reveal a dazzling heap of gold — monstrous nuggets, gold coins, Pre-Columbian gold objects — along with loose gemstones, carved necklaces, and a packet of thousand and five hundred dollar bills.

"Go ahead," he said, "pick up a nugget."

ix

I reached in and picked up a massive raw nugget the size of a hen's egg, cold and heavy. There is something atavistic about gold that thrills the imagination, and as I hefted it I felt my pulse quicken.

"That's from the Yukon," he said. "Nuggets that large are rare, worth three to four times their bullion value."

He reached in and removed the bills.

"What are those? Funny money?"

"No. It's legal United States tender"— not normally used in circulation, he said, but sometimes these large denomination notes were exchanged between banks to keep their accounts in balance. It wasn't hard to obtain one; he simply called his bank and ordered it, and a week later it arrived. He tucked the packet back in the chest. The chest also included a vital piece of paper which he showed me: an IOU for $100,000 drawn on his bank, so that he would know the chest was found when the discoverer collected the IOU. He rummaged around in the chest and brought out a handful of gold coins — beautiful old St. Gaudens double eagle gold pieces, along with dazzling gemstones, a 17th century Spanish emerald, and a gold Inca frog.

"Lift the chest. See how heavy it is."

I grasped it by the sides and could lift it only with difficulty. The total weight of gold and chest was more than forty pounds.

Forrest then explained what it was all about. After his cancer diagnosis, he had begun thinking of his own mortality. The doctors told him there was an eighty percent chance the cancer would return and kill him. So he had worked out a plan: when the cancer came back, he

X

would travel to a secret place he had identified and bring with him the treasure chest. In that place he would conceal himself and the treasure, and then and there end his life. He would leave behind a poem containing clues to where he was interred with the chest. Whoever was clever enough to figure out the poem and find his grave was welcome to rob it and take the treasure for themselves.

The final clue, he said, would be where they found his car: in the parking lot of the Denver Museum of Nature and Science.

He had worked out all the logistics but one: how he could pull this off by himself, without help. He did not feel he could entrust anyone else to assist him. "Two people can keep a secret," he said, "only if one of them is dead." He had already written the poem, and he now brought it out and read it to me. It was similar to the poem he later published in his book, The Thrill of the Chase, but not, if I recollect, exactly the same. He tweaked it many times over the years, making it harder.

I said that there were a lot of smart people out there and I feared the poem would be deciphered quickly and the treasure found in a week. But he assured me that the poem, while absolutely reliable if the nine clues were followed in order, was extremely difficult to interpret — so tricky that he wouldn't be surprised if it took nine hundred years before someone cracked it.

When first I heard his plan, I was astonished and amazed. I didn't really believe it. But the more time I spent with Forrest, the more I realized he was dead serious — no pun intended. I also realized it would make a marvelous movie: the story of a wealthy man who did take it with him. I pitched the idea to Lynda Obst, a classmate of mine from Pomona College, who had become a hugely successful Hollywood producer (Flashdance, Contact, Sleepless in Seattle). She loved the idea and asked me to write a treatment. When I called Forrest to make sure this was okay and offered to share the proceeds, he gave me his blessing, generously and firmly refused to accept any money, and made me promise only to invite him to the premiere — and the Oscars, if it got that far. I wrote a treatment and sold it to Lynda Obst Productions and 20th Century Fox. While the movie was never made (option available!) I did write a novel based on the idea, called The Codex, which featured a wealthy Santa Fe art dealer and collector who is dying of cancer and decides to take his fortune with him. He buries himself and his fabulous wealth in a secret tomb at the farthest ends of the earth, and he issues a challenge to his three lazy, no-good sons: if they want their inheritance, they have to find his tomb — and rob it.

As the years went by, I visited Forrest many times and saw the treasure in his vault. He often took things out and put other things in; he removed the currency, fearing it might rot; and he swapped out some of the gems for more gold coins and ancient Chinese jade faces. He also took out the IOU, he said, "because I thought my bank might not still be there when the chest was found." He had worked out a better way, he told me, to know when the treasure is discovered, but he has not shared that secret with me.

And then finally, one lovely summer day in August 2010, I visited him and he brought me into the vault. The chest was gone! "I finally hid it," he said. He was about to turn eighty years old and still in excellent health with no sign of cancer, and he decided to stop waiting and hide the chest now. This way was better, because he would be around to appreciate and enjoy the ensuing hunt.

And that, as everyone knows, was the beginning of what has developed into possibly the greatest treasure hunt of the 21st century. As I write this, seven of those nine hundred years have passed, a hundred thousand people have looked for the treasure, and three have lost their lives in the search — and yet it still remains out there somewhere, secreted in a dark and wild place, waiting to be found.

This treasure story is emblematic of who Forrest is — a war hero, a man of great generosity, and a truly original human being who lives life to the fullest, does things his own way, and doesn't worry too much about what others might think. Forrest is, above all, a creator and a teller of amazing stories. In this book he tells thirty-nine of the best of those stories, all true, with a note of commentary at the end of each one. They run the gamut from the inspiring and philosophical to the amusing and fabulous. These stories are a treasure of another kind, and some of them — who knows?— may contain more clues to the location of the real treasure.

I have read these stories with enormous pleasure, interest and enlightenment, and I hope you will enjoy them too.

teen Dollars a Square Inch   A PERSONAL TRIBUTE TO ERIC SLOANE   FENN

The Thrill of the Chase   *A Memoir*

too far to walk

TEEPEE SMOKE

LEON GASPARD   The Call of Distant F

The Thrill of the Chase   *A Memoir*

PREFACE

Many of the 40 chapters in this book were published on a blog where exposure to the public was minimal. All of the stories have been revised by me, and graphics changed, or added.

My personal reminiscences are told as I remember them happening. If my enthusiasm for storytelling should occasionally bend contrary to a circumstance, I hope the reader will know that the fault line lies within the failures of my 88-year-old memory, and not with the desires of my heart.

The first issue of this book was published in 2017 and went out of print in less than a year. I added a new story in this edition. It is the last chapter in my final book. Now it is time for me to rest.

TABLE OF CONTENTS

2
Supplemental Punishment

6
The Long Jump

10
Sweet Fragrances

20
An Education from Stanley

26
The Loom of the Desert

30
Me and Little Beaver

34
Shelling Corn

38
Experiences with Joe

44
Glory is Never Enough

46
Explosion on 3rd Street

52
Divorce Logic

56
Once in a While
I Do Something Right

62
Annabella's Hat

66
I Never Go Shopping, But…

70
The Unfortunate Hiccup

72
In a Tuck

76
Rainy Night Blessings

80
The Quahada Chief
on a Black Pony

86
The Prince of the Comancheros

92
Montana Golden

see page 46!

BOOM

96
Remnants of the Past

100
Things I Covet

104
Well, Here's Moses

106
Salute to a Warrior

110
The Iron Rooster
of Santa Fe County

114
Lessons from Forrest

118
Memories that Never Die

124
Me and Mummy Joe

128
Algernon's Relative

134
Cultures on Top of Cultures

136
The Evolution
of My Art Opinion

142
Doug Hyde in Stone

148
Apaches in the Garage

152
Me and Michael Douglas

154
Is It My Candy Ann?

156
The Graciella Experience

162
Partying with Suzanne Somers

168
The Bullet Comes Home

172
The Price of Freedom

176
Me and Dizzy Dean

1

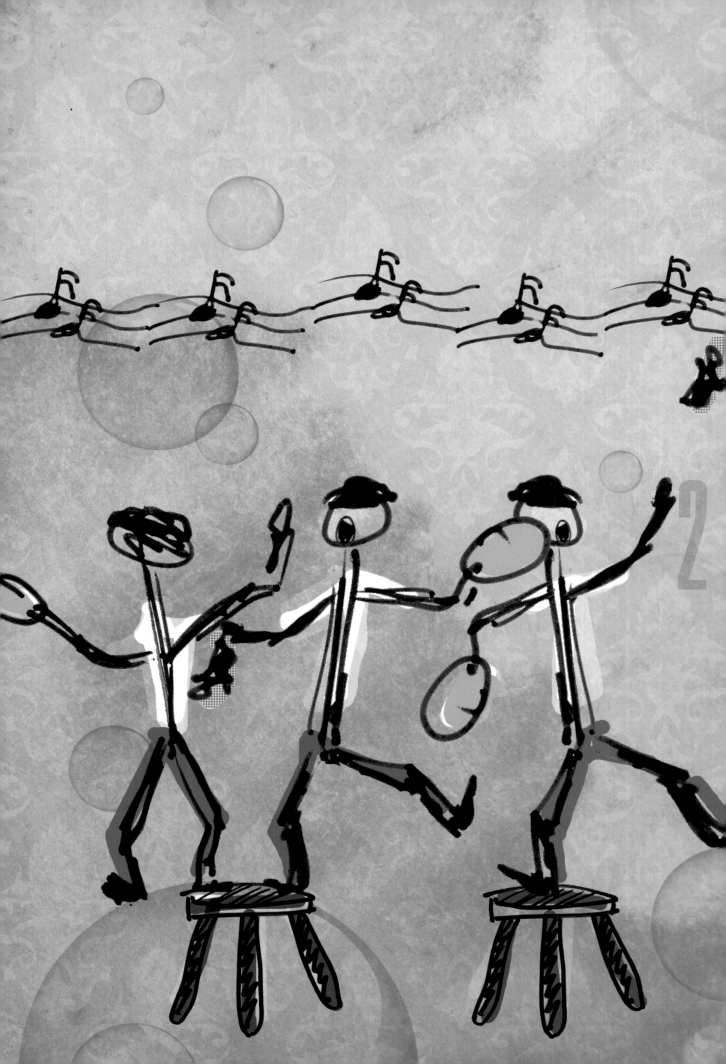

SUPPLEMENTAL PUNISHMENT

3

I just put my toothbrush in the dishwasher, so I have a few minutes to talk about how I turned one of life's great negatives into something positive.

In the late 1930s, I was in junior high school and, discounting my grades, life was mostly fun. But whenever my father caught me doing something that he thought was "inconsiderate," like putting itching powder in my brother's shorts, for example, he'd give me a spanking. The thought of the punishment was worse than the sting though, because I'd learned to keep two hankies in each of my back pockets just in case.

But when I locked my little sister out of the bathroom, my father became somewhat irate. After the customary whipping, believing I could benefit from some supplemental punishment, I was assigned the lone chore of doing the dreaded supper dishes. There were five in our family, so when you threw in the smelly gravy pan, rolling pin, and potato masher, the task was daunting.

While standing on a stool, washing a plate in front of the kitchen sink, determined not to let ill fortune best me, I suddenly broke into song. (My memory has faded during the 78 years that have ensued since then, but I remember starting with an aria from *La Bohème*,

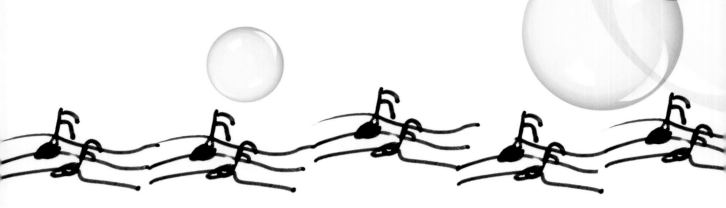

or some other great opera.) There, in the most domestic of settings, I pretended to be on an international stage, performing before kings and queens, and tsars and tsarinas. What the top of my voice lacked in quality, it made up for in decibels.

My family quickly exited the kitchen.

As words charged from my tongue the crescendo built in equal proportions to my enthusiasm, and the fanfare of waving a wet dishcloth back and forth only enhanced my stage presence. It was exhilarating. Our neighbors probably enjoyed my performance clear down to Nugent Avenue. (My father later admitted that I performed *Oh Sole Mio* with uncommon aplomb.)

But soon, to my horror, the dishes were all done and put away, and I wasn't even finished with my concert. Jolted by this sudden realization, I looked around, desperate for something else to wash… a stray fork, or maybe a misplaced pot lid. Failing that, I accepted that all good things must come to an end, and turned to bow to my audience — the icebox, the waffle iron, and the garbage can; all of which must have felt a little overwhelmed by my world-class presentation. With a beaming smile on my face, I exited stage left with the knowledge that victory had been brilliantly snatched from the jaws of defeat.

After that incident I frequently helped Mom with the dishes, but it was always by choice. My father never again assigned those duties to me as punishment.

Oops, the dishwasher just stopped, gotta go. **f**

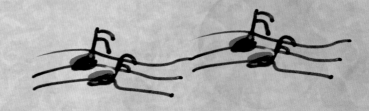

I would be the world's greatest singer if it were not for a lack of talent. There is ample motivation, but I practice only when I'm alone. I sense some progress, but being almost deaf may disqualify me as a judge.

5

Thank you!
Thank you very much!

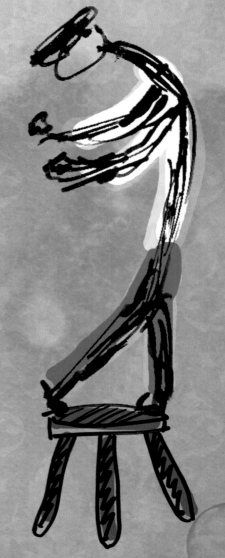

THE LONG JUMP

Kacir

Scotty

Paul

Edard

Laurens

It was a huge monster of an iron-looking thing – the bridge I mean – and I hated it with a passion. It crossed the Leon River on State Road 53, about six miles west of Temple, Texas, where I was born and raised.

Well, it wasn't actually the bridge itself that bothered me, but rather the 55-foot drop to the water, and I'll tell you why.

The cadre of friends I ran around with in high school was a pseudo-macho bunch. There was Edard, Kacir, Scotty, Paul Emery, Laurens, as well as several others who sat on the close periphery of our small group. They were all good guys and we were close, which is what made it so hard for me to be left standing up there all alone on that bridge after everyone else had jumped off.

I was going to do it right up until I looked down and heard some-one say that submerged logs sometimes lurked just under the surface and if you landed on one it would break both of your legs.

"Let's go!" they yelled, and all of them jumped. I couldn't believe it. All of a sudden they were just gone and I wasn't. How do you think that made a 16-year-old, 138 pound kid feel?

I knew what they were thinking, "It was a test for toughness and Fenn's tail fell out." I could just see them telling every good-looking girl in the whole junior class. It was a catastrophic moment for me and I felt terrible. My value shouldn't be diminished just because those guys couldn't see my real worth, should it?

It preyed on me, but for only a week or so. I felt my courage was only an inch too short to be long enough, so I developed a plan that was indelible in my mind. I'd show those guys.

On a cold, moonless night at about 3 a.m., I stole out of my bedroom window, jumped in my '35 Plymouth, and drove out State Road 53. My mind was made up and nothing could stop me. No one was around so I parked on the bridge, stepped out of my car, and looked down. I couldn't see the water but I knew it was down there somewhere. My pulse was tingling but without a second's hesitation, I climbed over the rail, fully clothed, and jumped. I just did it, and that was that. After what seemed like an hour I hit the water with a hard, cold splash.

When I surfaced my whole world had changed, and I was so proud. I started laughing with an insane sense of empowerment. I really showed those guys, and ha, I did it at night! "Just wait'll the news gets out," I thought.

I was wet and frozen when I climbed back in my bedroom window. I dried off, crawled into bed, and with a smug sense of satisfaction, I laid there thinking. Why should I even tell anyone? They probably wouldn't believe me anyway. Besides, the power of what I did would be subjugated a little if they knew. So I decided to keep it to myself.

Looking back now, I think maybe I grew up a little on a dark night 71 years ago on that great Leon River Bridge. | f

MY TWO SENSE

Jumping from the Leon River Bridge taught me that accomplishing difficult tasks sometimes requires only a simple mental adjustment.

ERVIEW
ugh truss bridge over
h River on FM 817 in
on

CATION
on, Bell County, TX

TUS
n to traffic

TORY
1939

SIGN
er through truss

MENSIONS
th of largest span:
1 ft
l length: 412.1 ft
width: 24.0 ft
cal clearance above
: 15.7 ft

COGNITION
ed to the National
ister of Historic Places
Oct. 10, 1996

O CALLED
o Road Bridge

ROXIMATE
TITUDE,
NGITUDE
6639, -97.44222
imal degrees)
59" N, 97°26'32" W
rees°minutes'seconds")

ADRANGLE MAP
on

ENTORY
MBERS
NBI 090140001505060
as bridge number on
National Bridge
entory)
HP 96001119 (National
ister of Historic Places
rence number)

PECTION
of 04.2013)
condition rating:
factory (6 out of 9)
erstructure condition
ng: satisfactory
ut of 9)
tructure condition
ng: satisfactory
ut of 9)
raisal: functionally
lete
ciency rating: 63.6 (out
o)

ERAGE
LY TRAFFIC
of 2011) 3,000

me

bay leaves

rosemary

oregano

smells bizarre & strong

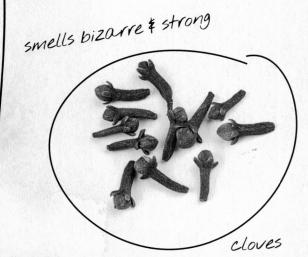

cloves

poppy seeds

thyme

SWEET FRAGRANCES

It's blustery outside and my wife went out grocery shopping, so I decided to revisit a fun time I had when I was a kid. My mom let me smell different spices and herbs as she stirred them into recipes she was preparing. I enjoyed the interaction with her, and the wrinkles on my nose indicated how much I liked or disliked each aroma.

Just so you'll know the difference; spices are dried seed, root, fruit, bark or vegetable substances. Herbs are seeds, roots, leaves, flowers, resin, and berries. OK?

Anyway, that got me thinking about my wife's metal spice drawer, so I took it out of the cabinet to have a look inside. It was heavy and I rested it on our kitchen table, but when I sat down and pulled that thing toward me, something sharp on the bottom scraped a gash into the wooden tabletop. I'll try to fix it with wax before she gets home. I hate when those things happen and I can't blame them on my dog.

There were 72 round bottles in the drawer and each was about four inches tall. I read the labels and sniffed the contents of every jar, and then stuck my finger in each spice to taste the flavors. It's funny how some smell so different from the way they taste. If you don't believe me, just go in the pantry and smell your vanilla. You'll love it enough to take another whiff, but don't take a taste, and that's fair warning.

I quickly learned that some spices smell like others, so I don't know why a cook needs so many different kinds. Most didn't make much of an impression, but here are some notes and observations about those that did.

TURKISH GROUND CUMIN

"Use on Middle Eastern & Mexican dishes." They say it's a "must," but it doesn't do much for me. If I ever try any Middle Eastern dishes I probably won't like them. I love Mexican food but I'm not going to put this stuff on my enchiladas.

CLOVES

Smells bizarre and strong. The taste has a bite that comes with a lasting sting. It took three seconds to feel the full impact of the flavor on my tongue. It was terrible. I felt jaundiced and had to suck on an ice cube. Stay away from cloves — that's my advice. Are you sure it's something to eat and not some kind of disinfectant?

OREGANO

The label is supposed to say what it is but it doesn't, so I don't trust it completely. I think you put it on spaghetti, but maybe not. Oregano has a bitter taste and it numbed my tongue a little. I know it's used on pizza. I like pizza if it has pepperoni, cheese, bell peppers, onions, anchovies, and oregano on it.

12

SPICES

ground cumin

paprika

the label doesn't say what it is
but something in there is dead.

cayenne pepper

turmeric

lemon pepper

mace

POPPY SEEDS

"Ancient civilizations used them to add color and texture to food." Yeah, I know what's made out of poppy seeds and it doesn't need color or texture. It might be embarrassing to have this little jar in my house if the drug enforcement guys come nosing around. I'll speak with my wife about it.

MACE

Its smell is stronger than it's taste. Makes me suspicious. "Use on puddings and spinach," it says. I think the person who wrote that may have been sniffing poppy seeds. It says mace grows on the same trees as nutmeg and it tastes warm. OK, I like things that taste warm.

GARLIC POWDER

When I unscrewed the top, fine white powder spilled all over my lap. It smelled like something that might rust the lid. I don't like garlic unless it's on toasted bread and I'm eating spaghetti. But it's fun to grow in my garden because it's educational to watch.

CLOVES

Another jar. Why would anyone want two full jars of cloves?

ANISE SEEDS

These are cute little gray seeds but hard to bite. They taste like licorice. The label says something about pastries but it's faded and I can't read more. It's probably okay. When I was a kid people tried to give me soft sticks of licorice. They came in black and an ugly reddish-maroon color. Maybe that's why I didn't like licorice then. I probably still don't.

14

PAPRIKA

I can't tell if I like it or not. It's the "Ground dried pod of the sweet chili pepper." That's what the label says but I really don't care one way or the other. "Mix lemon juice, celery, crab, and mayonnaise together and spoon into hollowed tomatoes, or use as a sandwich spread." Sounds like something they serve in expensive restaurants. Not for me, but thanks anyway.

CAYENNE

"A dash awakens dips, soups, salads, sauces, and entrees." Awakens? Maybe that's a typo. I used to like a little cayenne pepper on Texas chili but haven't tried it in a while. Maybe I should stop reading the labels.

LEMON PEPPER

I absolutely love Lemon Pepper. It's made of ground lemon peel and "hardy coarse-ground pepper." It's good on grilled steaks and hamburgers. They say it has riboflavin in it for color. I can't imagine why anyone would want to add color to a hamburger. Sometimes I sprinkle a little lemon pepper on my arm and lick it. All of my grandkids think I'm weird, except maybe little Piper.

ALLSPICE

It's made from the berries of evergreen trees but it smells a little like cloves. I don't dare taste it. When the label suggested that I put it on squash that was enough for me. I screwed the green lid back on that jar and hid it at the bottom of the pile. I wonder if my neighbor would like to have it.

allspice

pickling spice

not much smell

ground cardamon

nutmeg

garlic powder

celery salt

GROUND TURMERIC

"Belongs to the ginger family." I don't want to talk about it. The label doesn't say what it is but something in there is dead. Google says its active ingredient is curcumin and it's used to treat cancer. You probably need a prescription to buy it. I'm throwing this stuff out fast. I think I need to speak with my wife again.

PICKLING SPICE

"Use with boiling beets, sour beef, pickling and cabbage." I just don't know what to say. I'll bet someone's making a fortune with these things.

GROUND CARDAMOM

This one is pungent. "You can add it to hamburgers and espresso." I would never use it on either. I use onions when I want something pungent and I don't drink espresso. It's a drink for girls.

ROSEMARY

You should sprinkle it on the charcoal just before you start grilling the chicken. That's an herb? I don't like it because it reminds me of a girl I used to know. She threw rocks at me one day when I was walking home from school and I never forgot it. Heck with her.

THYME

This one has a funny name and a routine aroma. "It is the essence of French cooking and is used as a background flavor." Background flavor? What does that mean? "It's good with creamed onions." I don't like creamed onions. In fact, I don't like French cooking and I feel better having said that. I think the French believe they invented food. "Thyme was the symbol of courage in ancient Greece." Now I remember why I'm not a chef.

CELERY SALT

Very salty and tastes like celery. I like both so I guess it's OK. The Indians may have used it to help tan skins.

WHOLE NUTMEGS

They look like small pecans before you take the hulls off. Not much smell. You're supposed to grate them on top of hot chocolate and things like that. I may try it later tonight. It will impress my wife so long as she doesn't look closely at her kitchen table top.

BAY LEAVES

These smell good and look like plain old leaves to me. They're about three inches long and crisp to the bite. "Hand gathered from bay laurel trees and carefully dried to ensure superior quality." I wonder why they have to be careful, they're just leaves. You're supposed to cook them in soups and other things but remove them before you serve the dish. I would sure hope so.

CLOVES

Why does my wife have three bottles of cloves?

ARROWROOT POWDER

"Easily digested – may be substituted for cornstarch." If that's true then why would anyone buy cornstarch, which is more expensive? I think this spice company should be investigated.

My favorites are Lemon Pepper and Ground Saigon Cinnamon. I don't remember any of these spices from when I was a kid. Maybe I'll just stick with sea salt, black pepper, and Tabasco.

I hear my wife pulling into the garage so I need to hurry and get the wax. I wonder if she bought another jar of cloves. f

18

my table scratch

I really liked hanging around the kitchen with my mom. Wouldn't it be nice if all of us could go back and do some of that again?

AN EDUCATION FROM STANLEY

21

When I came home from Vietnam I was mentally and physically exhausted. That's the truth of it. I'd flown 328 combat missions in 348 days, lost a roommate, and was shot down twice. With a primary duty of running the command post, it seemed I had been working all the time. I lost 22 pounds and hadn't even realized it.

Spending a wide-eyed night in the Laotian jungle waiting to be rescued gave me time to think. I decided there had to be something better than that and I was ready for it. So I turned down a promotion to Lieutenant Colonel and got out of the Air Force.

Two diabolically opposed thoughts were stirring in the back of my mind. I had a family to feed, which was paramount, but I wasn't going to wear a watch, a coat and tie, or shoes that had to be shined. And an alarm clock was not going to rest on the night stand beside my bed. That meant I had to have my own business, and I wanted one where our average customer gave us $2,500 or more.

So my wife and I moved our two young daughters to Santa Fe and jumped into the art gallery business with hurried steps. We plastered the walls during the day and slept on the floor

Photograph (at left)
by Lisa Law

at night. We built an art foundry and started casting Western art bronzes. Since our ambitions didn't come with instructions, we alternated between having successful energetic impulses and going limp when a great idea didn't work out.

I wanted to sell expensive art, but we didn't have any. Then one day, a Persian rug with wefts made of 18 carat gold thread was consigned to us. The former owner was the Shah of Iran. It was so heavy that four men were needed to carry it into our gallery, and so valuable that three armed guards sat beside it around-the-clock in eight hour shifts. We didn't sell it, but we got the first faint smell of what life could be like in the fast lane, which was where we wanted to be. We were learning fast, and valuable experiences were coming in rapid succession.

Signs were placed in each of our five display rooms that said, "Please touch, we are responsible," and our policy was to take anyone's check for any amount of money. Those were good decisions because it told our clients who we were, and they appreciated it.

The two alligators in the pond beside our gallery were a draw, as was my little dog who followed me everywhere. My lack of education and business experience began paying dividends.

After a while, we started making payroll out of our accounts receivable. That was one way of measuring the business. We began to feel good, but a question kept gnawing on my mind. Why would anyone pay $65,000 for an oil painting by Nicolai Fechin when a great print of that same painting could be had for just $150? Is there a difference between art and art?

22

Print of painting by Nicolai Fechin, oil painting by Nicolai Fechin (inset).

The answer of course is ego; the joy of owning an original. I knew that, but I still couldn't reconcile the idea in my mind. One day, I explained my feelings on the subject to Stanley Marcus, who was one of the world's great businessmen. "Forrest," he said, "Two women are walking down the street together wearing identical full-length mink coats. One was purchased at J.C. Penney for $3,500, and the other came from Neiman Marcus for $12,500. Can you look at them and tell which is wearing the Neiman Marcus?" I felt like a beer drinker at a champagne tasting.

"I can," he said. "The lady wearing our label carries herself with more pride and confidence, and she isn't afraid to look strangers in the eye and say hello. On occasion someone will sew our label into the neck of a Penney's coat, but it doesn't come with the 'Neiman's feeling,' and she knows it. Don't you see?"

It was great business advice. All of a sudden I didn't want prints hanging anywhere around my house or gallery. **f**

MY TWO SENSE

In 1952 Stanley introduced a new tradition of selling extravagant and unusual gifts in the annual Neiman Marcus Christmas catalog. They included a 20-million-dollar submarine, his and her's airplanes, and a live tiger.

THE LOOM
OF THE
DESERT

IDAH MEACHAM STROBRIDGE

THE LOOM OF THE DESERT

Once in a while I happen upon someone who is wonderfully different. Idah Meacham Strobridge is one such person. Her book *The Loom of the Desert*, published in 1907, demonstrates a certain classiness that I wish all books had. One-thousand copies were printed in a limited edition, and mine is autographed and numbered 189. Idah tipped in seven photos, with a wonderful calligraphic hand, and ink lettered each caption.

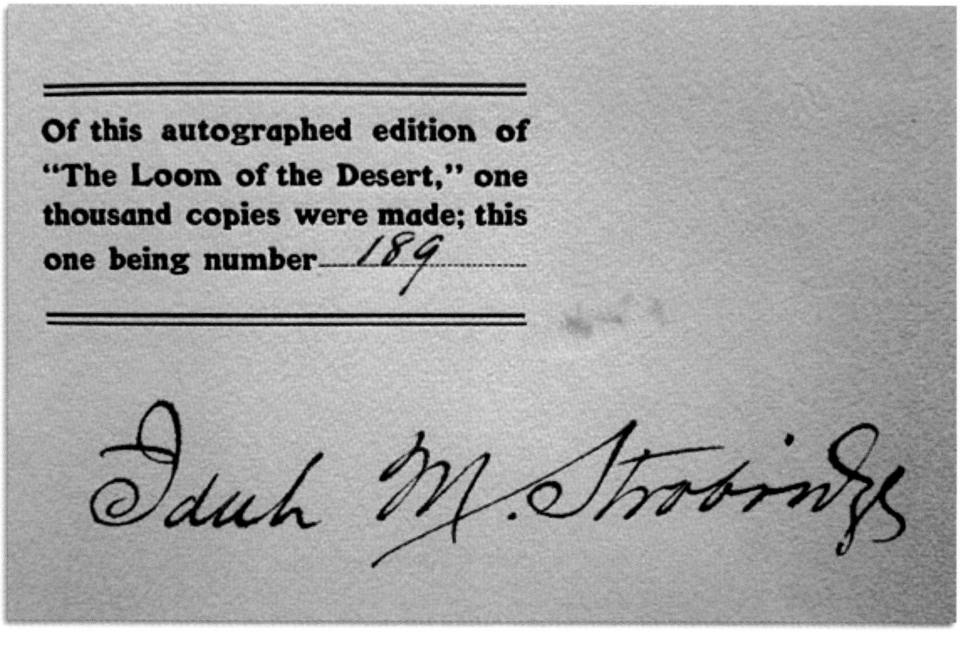

Of this autographed edition of "The Loom of the Desert," one thousand copies were made; this one being number___189___

Idah M. Strobridge

and swift"

Dear Fred,

Now I'm going away, and I am to stay a year. The money will last us two about that long & I ask Mr. Beard to go with me, so you needn't blame him. I ain't got nothing against you, only you wouldn't never take me nowheres; and I just couldn't stan it no longer. I've been a good wife, and worked hard, and earned money for you, but I ain't never had none of it myself to spend. So I'm goin to have it now; for some of it is mine anyway. It has been work–work all the time, and you wouldn't take me nowheres. So I'm a going now myself. I don't like Mr. Beard better than I do you – that ain't it and if you want me to come back to you in a year I will. And I'll be a good wife to you again, like I was before. Only you needn't expect me to say I'll be sorry because I done it, for I won't be I won't never be sorry I done it; never never! So, good-by.

Your loving wife,
Martha F. Scott

29

I found this little volume for ten dollars, languishing and over-looked on a paint-peeled wooden shelf in a forgettable bookstore somewhere. It was rebound from my own pocket; money I very much enjoyed spending.

This is Idah's forward to *The Loom*…

There, in that land set apart for Silence, and Space, and the Great Winds, Fate — a grim, still figure — sat at her loom weaving the destinies of desert men and women. The shuttles shot to and fro without ceasing, and into the strange web were woven the threads of Light, and Joy, and Love; but more often were they those of Sorrow, or Death, or Sin. From the wide Gray Waste the Weaver had drawn the color and design; and so the fabric's warp and woof were of the desert's tone. Keeping this always well in mind will help you the better to understand those people of the plains, whose lives must needs be often sombrehued. (How do you like that word?)

Beginning on page 18 of Idah's book is a tale about Martha Scott. Lasting only 12 pages, it relates the story of a woman who perhaps epitomizes many rural women of her day. Let me read you one chapter (see opposite page).

That is my book review for today. You can get reprints on AbeBooks-.com for under $9, and 1st editions for a little more money than that. f

FORREST
MY TWO SENSE
12 SEP

Idah lost three sons at an early age, followed by her husband. Maybe that's why she was able to write in such technicolor tones.

ME AND LITTLE BEAVER

In 1938, a new comic strip called *Red Ryder* appeared in the newspapers. It was about a crime-fighting cowboy who wore a white hat and rode a fast horse. Little Beaver was his young Indian sidekick, and I dreamed of riding with them through the mountain passes as we chased bad guys wearing black hats. My name was Luke Revolver, and every time I saw a man wearing a black hat I'd tell Little Beaver to watch out.

Each panel in the cartoon had a taste for overstatement and seemed to bounce at me with six-gun bluster. It was great make-believe. That's when I was eight.

That same year, my father bought me a Daisy Air Rifle. It had "Red Ryder" burned in big letters across the wooden stock. I liked it so much I kept it under my covers at night, loaded and ready for action.

The gun could hold about 250 BBs and it fired without making much noise. That meant I could shoot again if I missed a meadow lark the first time. Meadow larks don't like noise, and I needed to get five on Saturdays so each member in my family could have meat for supper.

About 40 years later I met Fred Harman, who drew the *Red Ryder* cartoons. With 750 newspapers and 40 million readers, it was the largest syndicated comic strip in the country.

In later years, Fred became an important cowboy artist whose work sold for a lot of money. When our gallery advertised one of his paintings with a full-page, color ad in *Apollo* magazine, he came in to thank me. I used the opportunity to show him my old BB gun. He told me that the Daisy Company gave him a 5-cent royalty for every gun they sold with his Red Ryder logo on the cheek plate. Sometimes success comes in small denominations.

I related to Fred Harman. He was a link to my hunting days as a small boy in Texas and to Red Ryder, with whom I rode vicariously across the prairie looking for rustlers.

I have willed my BB gun to my grandson, Shiloh, and he had better be careful what he shoots with it. Little Beaver might be watching. | f

my BB gun, 1938 vintage

There's a Fred Harmon Museum in Pagosa Springs, Colorado. I recommend it. Fred was a founding member of the Cowboy Artists of America, and I remember him as a friendly man with a bushy mustache that moved about when he talked. His grinning face always set me at ease. Over his lifetime he painted thousands of cowboys, but I always thought their legs were too short.

MY TWO SENSE

FOR FIRST

5 FEB

1938

SHELLING CORN

My old friend Keri recently sent me a full-page color magazine ad that our gallery ran in 1978. It advertised *Shelling Corn*, a large oil painting by Joseph Henry Sharp. It depicts Elkfoot Jerry Maribal and Crucita, two Taos Indians sitting on a banco by the fireplace in the artist's studio.

The ad conjured up old memories from my 17 years as a gallery owner in Santa Fe, and I can recall the entire history of that painting. Well, maybe not the entire history, but I'll tell you what I know.

It was painted in Taos about 1925-35, I'd guess, but it could be a little earlier. I gave a local family $55,000 for it. They obtained it from the artist in trade for Navajo weavings. I sold the painting for $65,000 to an old friend. When he wanted to buy a yacht, his wife made him sell it back to me for $75,000. Later, we sold it to a good client in Blue Bell, Pennsylvania for $150,000. When he passed away, the director of the Los Angeles Athletic Club acquired it for $250,000 and sold it for $750,000. It sold again for 1.5 million and then again for I don't know what. Not bad appreciation for just 20 years or so.

I interviewed Jerry Maribal in 1980 while researching my Sharp biography. Jerry was 104 years old, and totally blind.

When I entered the darkened room Jerry was reclining on his bed. He smiled and said, "I'm happy to see you, Mr. Fenn."

Meeting Elkfoot Jerry Maribal was a mind-expanding experience for me. He said interesting things about his early life at Taos Pueblo and about his relationship with Mr. Sharp. In his quiet way he spoke through the haze of faraway memories while I mostly listened, not wanting to interrupt him with the weakness of my own thoughts. As I left his room his granddaughter said, "The leaves will soon fall from the apricot tree." I thought that was such a beautiful thing to say. Mr. Maribal died the next morning, and out of respect, the pueblo was closed to all outsiders for three days.

I can't say that Elkfoot Jerry was a friend because we met only that one time. It was remiss of me for not meeting him sooner. And why didn't I also meet Hunting Son, Soaring Eagle, Crucita, Standing Deer, Leaf Down, Agapito, George Eats Alone, Lady Pretty Blanket, Adalina, Wolf Ear, Strikes His Enemy Pretty, Mary Tailfeather, Shows A Fish, Medicine Crow, White Swan, Takes A Wrinkle, Julia Sun Goes Slow, Shorty White Grass, Naked Alberto, Hairy Moccasin, Albidia, Bawling Deer, and a host of other Indians who also posed for Mr. Sharp? Many of those names may have gained some romance through translation, but don't you love it? f

36

Photograph of Jerry Maribal
by Joseph Henry Sharp

CAPTAIN AMERICA
MARCH
No. 1
COMIC
45 thrilling pages of CAPTAIN AMERICA
PLUS OTHER GREAT FEATURES!
U.S. MUNITIONS WORKS
SMASH
THRU CAP
AMERIC
CAME FAC
FACE W
HITLER
Also
CAPTAIN
AMERICA'S
YOUNG ALLY
BUCKY

EXPERIENCES WITH JOE

39

During my late pre-teen years, I was really into reading funny books. They weren't funny, but that's what they were called. Later, they were renamed comic books, but I will never subscribe to that unfortunate change.

Across the street from my house, down on the corner of French and Main, was a man who distributed magazines. Many of the publishers sent their periodicals to him, and then he'd deliver them around town to every newsstand. It was a small mom-and-pop operation.

At the end of each month, the cover of every unsold magazine would be removed so they could be sent back to their respective publishers for credit.

The person who made that happen was an elderly black man named Joe. I absolutely loved that old man, and I'd often go over to see him after school. We'd talk about all sorts of things while I helped him tear covers. His grandparents had been slaves, and his tales of picking cotton on the Mississippi river bottoms were right out of Mark Twain. When I told him I'd like to have worked alongside him in the fields, he said, "Hush boy, you froth too much," or words to that effect. Funny that I would remember that about him.

Occasionally, I would beg Joe to let me take a couple of unsold funny books home for the night. I didn't care if the covers had been torn off. The retail price was a dime, and I couldn't afford even one. But since he had to take all of the unsold magazines to the dump, and would get in trouble if he couldn't account for each one, I'd read them at night and return them the next morning before school. I had many funny book heroes, but my favorites were *Sub-Mariner* and *Captain America*.

Joe, whose life experiences extended past both extremes of work and hardship, lived alone in a single room that had an unshaded light bulb hanging from the ceiling. His space was so small that he sat on his bed while he worked. Joe was fluent about life on the foggy shores of civilization and I was thirsty to learn what he knew.

He told of being in a store in Hillsboro, Texas while it was robbed by Bonnie and Clyde. As the gangsters fled, a piece of paper fell from Bonnie's coat pocket. On it was a poem she had written. Joe picked it up and kept it all of these years. He pulled the crumpled paper from his Bible and let me see it. It wasn't worth reading, but I think it was Joe's claim to immortality.

I never heard Joe complain, but maybe that was because he knew how to make things work. As a kid, he greased wagon wheels, and for a while he walked door-to-door in town trying to sell turkeys. When he was successful, he'd go buy one from a farmer on credit to fill the order, and then deliver it to his client for a small profit. As soon as he

40

received the money, he'd walk a few miles back to pay the farmer.

Occasionally my mom would bake a mincemeat pie for Joe and have me take it to him hot. They were his favorite, and once a month or so she'd invite him over for supper and we'd talk about things that were going on around the country.

I don't remember what happened to Joe because his memory has mostly faded into the rest of my life, but he was much more than just an asterisk in the family scrapbook of those years. He was a mentor to me at a time in my life when it mattered. His gentle nature and humble way still lingers in a corner of my mind. |f

42

MY TWO SENSE

It took me a while to realize how smart my elders were, especially people like Joe, my parents, and my football coach. They must have thought I was pretty dense. Now that I'm 87 years old, no one around me wants to listen to what I say. Maybe that's one reason I spend so much time alone. At least I like the company.

GLORY IS NEVER ENOUGH

45

I'm so proud of this football. It's a genuine Rawlings Pro 5 lace-up.

For two years, I was the 98-pound star quarterback for Central Junior High School Kittens, in Temple, Texas. With this very football I made my first and only touchdown. It was a one-yard dash through the middle of the line.

We were playing the Troy Warriors and my good friend, Edard, who was the center for our team, moved the opposing guard to the right just enough for me to plunge through. It was a daring feat of mental and physical dexterity. I'm sure the crowd was roaring and the *Temple Daily Telegram* probably would have reported it in headlines if someone had told them about the achievement. I don't remember who won the game, but Edard saved the football and presented it to me later.

In later life, while trying to avoid those who distract me from my self-esteem, I am always reminded of the heroic performances I committed on the football fields of my youth. f

46

EXPLOSION ON 3RD STREET

47

My brother Skippy never had a plan B because he always expected plan A to work. He functioned on the periphery where most kids his age, including me, didn't even think to look. But he couldn't control outside interferences forever.

When he was 17 years old, he started a New Year's firecracker business at the corner of 3rd Street and French in Temple, Texas. It was near the high school and next door to Smith's Drug Store. His good friend Leroy Calhoun, who had a few bucks saved up, became his partner.

School was out for the holidays, but all the kids were still hanging around the social soda fountain at Smith's, and waving past the firecracker stand.

On the second day, a couple of giggling girls walked up to flirt with the two enterprising business men. One purchased a fuse bomb, lit it, and tossed it over the counter at Leroy, thinking it would be a fun joke. The dangerous apparatus landed on some Areal Bombettes, and promptly detonated with a furious ricocheting blast that was heard clear down to the cemetery — two miles distant. The entire store

blown up Skippy

inventory of holiday explosives joined in the mighty discharge. A local newspaper reported that a box of dung fuse-lighters landed over by the school gymnasium.

Both Skippy and Leroy, with hairs afire, were blown onto 3rd Street's yellow center stripe. One observer lamented that tires were screeching as speeding cars careened through the burning debris and secondary explosions, trying to dodge human bodies and dangerous burning devices.

The first I knew about it was when my father ran out of our house and yelled, "Quick Bubba, get in the car, Skippy's been blown up!" When my brother saw us walk into the hospital room, his face lit up with a wide grin. It was easy to see how proud he was. But what a pitiful sight, with a blackened face and bandages covering his body. Father just shook his head as if to say, "Well, at least he's still alive."

Forrest, Peggy,
Irene, Skippy,
Donnie and June

Skippy's girlfriend, Irene Vance, stopped by to visit too. She brought her cousin with her, whom I had yet to meet. Her name was Peggy Jean Proctor.

Skippy eventually recovered and married Irene. Peggy and I started dating and were married eight years later. That was 64 years ago and almost nothing has changed, except Peggy has gotten prettier and I've gotten older, which must be one of Madam Nature's major design deficiencies.

Poor Leroy Calhoun was classified 4F as a result of the firecracker episode, and it prevented him from being drafted during the Korean War.

I've jammed a lot of oral history into these 509 words, but I've also left out a few things. Skippy trampled the grass around some pretty interesting events during his 50 years of life, and I was a tag-along observer with him for my share. I don't know who decided that we can't go back and do it all over again, but I don't subscribe to it. Can anyone help me? f

50

MY TWO SENSE
FORREST
4 JUL

I don't understand why anyone would buy firecrackers, moon rockets, or twirl-aways. They're expensive and dangerous, and last only a few seconds. A kid I knew once put a small cherry bomb in a tub of water and invited the girls to go over and look at it. It wasn't dangerous, but everyone sure got wet. I pretended to be appalled. Let's start celebrating the 4th of July by giving each other banana cream pies instead.

DIVORCE LOGIC

Back in the mid 1980s, I met a nice married couple at an opening in our art gallery. They were in their twenties, and people smiled at the sight of them walking around, holding hands, and munching on the finger foods we had near the wine cooler. In subsequent weeks I saw them infrequently around town, whispering to each other and holding hands.

I don't remember her name, so for some subliminal reason I'll call her Angel. She was walking toward me one day as I departed the bank on Palace Avenue. Her eyes were red, her hair was a gnarled muddle, and she was sobbing uncontrollably. I was startled by the sight of her.

We stopped to talk, and as she smeared a hankie across her face, she explained what a bad person her ex-husband was and that she would never recover from what he did to her. "It's been two months, you know." No, I didn't know, but that was okay.

After a long coffee respite at the Plaza Cafe, her emotions subsided somewhat. I learned that Angel was a professional potter who was trying to support herself in a failing market. I felt terrible, and wondered what I could do to help.

53 **Fred**

Finally, it came to me. I told her to go and make her divorce in the form of a pot because we were going to have a funeral for it. She started laughing and hugged me, and then laughed and hugged me some more. The spell of doom was broken and she hurried away to her studio.

Well, ten days later, I was digging a hole at the north end of Room Block 2 at San Lazaro Pueblo. It was beside a prehistoric path that led down to an ancient clay mine. Angel was sniffling into her hankie. It had been an awkward 45 minute drive.

She had made the ugliest pottery-thing I have ever seen. It was about 18 inches high, 10 inches across, and was littered with dismal, black figures with jagged edges. The iron nails that she had intermittently driven into that poor vessel were destroyed and crumbling as a result of the high-temperature firing. Angel had written her ex's name in big black letters, but I am sure it was misspelled. "Ferd," it said. I wondered what that was all about.

54

55

After she threw some personal things into the pot, I put the lid on, placed it reverently into the ground, and covered it up with dirt. Then she started piling rocks on the grave... and kept piling them on. I suppose maybe she was afraid that somehow her divorce would get out of the hole.

I decided to leave her alone to conduct the funeral, and walked back to wait in the car.

Well, I've never heard such carrying on. It was so loud! There was yelling and sobbing, singing and screaming, and spiteful maledictions. A few of the words she spat had definitions I was not even cognizant of. During one phase of the tantrum, I heard her scream "FRED!" — and that's about the same time the blossoms started falling from a nearby cholla cactus.

I quickly rolled my car windows up and considered the notion that maybe I should have been a therapist instead of an art dealer. f

MY TWO SENSE

It is fun to notice how quickly attitudes can change when the right stimuli is introduced to a situation. I can imagine that down through history, more than one fracas has been started because some big-shot's coffee wasn't hot enough, or someone's chicken got stolen.

56

ONCE IN A WHILE I DO SOMETHING RIGHT

Wilson Hurley was an artist (and a good one), and the price of his larger paintings frequently ran up to around $100,000. His father, Patrick Hurley, was ambassador to China during World War II. As a kid, Wilson travelled widely with his father and had personal letters from Generals MacArthur and Eisenhower. In 1945, Wilson graduated from West Point and became a pilot in the Air Force, serving as a forward air controller in Vietnam. He was entertaining in a conversation and we always had plenty to talk about.

Well, sometime in the 1980s, some guy ran a red light and hit Wilson's car. The jolt pinched a nerve in his neck and he was incapacitated – unable to paint for about a year. He couldn't make a living, so he sued, and it went to court in Albuquerque.

Since I had a gallery in Santa Fe and sold Wilson's paintings, I was called to testify as an expert witness about the value of his work, and how much money he lost by not being able to paint. I was duly sworn to tell the truth, the whole truth, and nothing but the truth. The judge broke with tradition and wore a blue robe – my favorite color. The scene was set with only a few spectators.

The problem was that I didn't like the defense attorney at first sight (or any other sight after that). His villainous face and bulging eyes made him look like Peter Lorre. I didn't know the jerk, but he was someone I very much enjoyed not caring for.

Well, most of the questions from the defense jerk's mouth came out reeking of sarcastic idioms that were aimed at discrediting me. He covertly insinuated that I was a derelict witness, not qualified to be on the stand. When one of my answers turned into a short dissertation, the jerk interrupted me. "Yes or no, Mr. Fenn, yes or no," he yelled in a croaky, belligerent voice. All of a sudden the court room became a very hostile environment and I was happily getting fed up with this guy. I just sat there as the lawyer's eyes captured me like a 40-pound turkey staring at a June bug.

I turned to the bench and said very apologetically, "Judge, I swore to tell the truth and the whole truth. If the defense attorney won't allow me to do that, then I must respectfully withdraw my oath." There was silence in the court as everyone sat stunned. The jerk looked like he'd just crawled out from under a garbage truck. I posed straight ahead and tried to stay collected, hoping the judge wouldn't cite me for contempt.

Finally he called the lawyers into his chambers, and as they disappeared and the door slammed, I relaxed. "It could go either way," I thought. Wilson was also a lawyer, and when he saw the jury feigning snickers, his frown turned to a smile. When the trial resumed, the judge said I could answer the questions as I pleased, and I was re-sworn

in. I ducked that bullet with impressive form. Wilson agreed.

Surely what I did was not only legal, but necessary, although I'd never heard of a witness un-swearing himself before. At lunch, I ordered iced tea, chicken fried steak with the gravy on the side, and no veggies. Wilson paid and left a nice tip. It had been a fun day. f

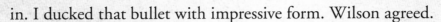

I like courtroom drama and that's why Matlock was one of my favorite TV programs. Gerry Spence, the great trial lawyer, has never lost a criminal case. He stayed in my guest house for a couple of days and we had some stimulating conversations. Something he said has stuck with me, "It's much better to have the best lawyer in the courtroom than to be innocent."

60

MY TWO SENSE
6 JUN
1980

ANNABELLA'S HAT

63

About 40 years ago – maybe more – an old Basque sheepherder came to me wanting to sell an awkward looking Alibates arrowhead. It was worth about five bucks, so when he said he wanted fifteen, I bought it. I couldn't guess how old the man was but his face looked like he'd slept on it for a long time.

"Where'd you find that point?" I asked.

"I dunno. Wherever I went, there I was," or words similar.

He had a fun way about him so we sat down. He pulled a folded half-sheet of newspaper from his back pocket, tore off a small square, and rolled a cigarette. The "tobacco" looked like cedar bark. Then, to my amazement, he struck an iron strike-a-light against a piece of flint, which caused a spark that lit his smoke. And he did it with one hand. I couldn't believe my eyes. I have a collection of fire starters and have used them at mountain man rendezvous, but would never have thought what he did was possible.

at left, strike-a-light

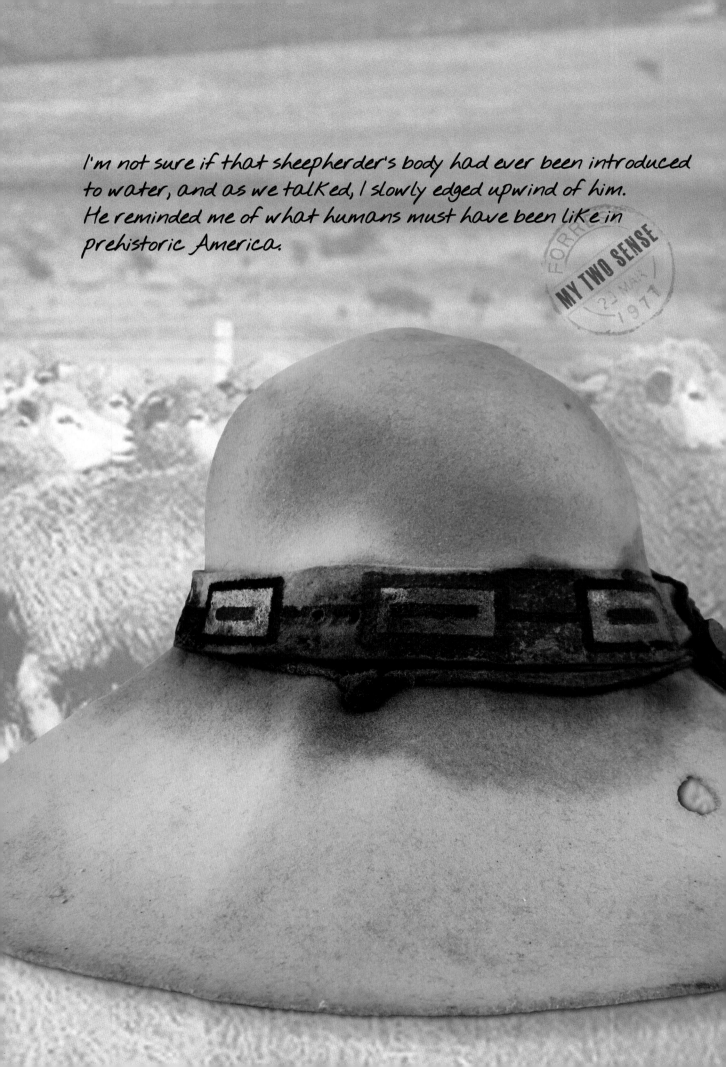

I'm not sure if that sheepherder's body had ever been introduced to water, and as we talked, I slowly edged upwind of him. He reminded me of what humans must have been like in prehistoric America.

Several cigarettes later, the sheepherder rested his hat on the bench next to me. I picked it up. It was homemade from very thick, hand-tanned hide (probably buffalo), and was maybe a hundred years old. He could see I liked it, and smiled to reveal an interesting tooth-lacking dental pattern.

"It'll break a fall," he grinned, and pointed to the bullet hole near the hat's forehead. "Got that one moonlit night when Anabella's husband showed up unexpectedly. Unreasonable man, he was," and the sheep man's expression said that it was a proud failing. It didn't take much for me to know that both the hat and the Basque had been molded in rude elements.

"How much you want for this worthless old beat up hat?" I asked.

"No sir, with its history of saving my life, a million dollars wouldn't buy that thing."

"I'll give you three hundred bucks."

"My God, sir, you sure bought a great hat."

And to this day, "that thing" is sitting on a table near my front door where I can brag about it to everyone who comes in my house. Some great objects just stand out above everything else. f

I NEVER GO SHOPPING, BUT...

67 there I was in Kaune's Neighborhood Market with five items in my pushcart. I was just picking up a few things that I needed in order to watch the Broncos play the Cowboys: pepperoni, bologna, salami, Tabasco, and horseradish.

As I approached the checkout counter, a shapely twentyish-looking woman raced past me. Her cart was loaded with six-packs of Corona beer. She wore short-shorts and slosh sandals, but it was her large hair – garish red and full of curlers – that struck me. The curlers were mostly white but a few were brown, and her piercings and tattoos introduced me to a world I had rarely seen before. "Mz. Fashion Maven," I thought. I told myself I had to get out more.

As I slowed my cart to prevent a wreck, our eyes met, and Mz. Maven gave me a grin that said my 87 years were no match for her youth and exuberance.

The checkout line moved slowly and the delay gave me plenty of time to observe Mz. Maven, who seemed to be growing annoyed by my preoccupation with the objects decorating her hair. As we stood there looking at each other, I politely asked, pointing to her updo,

"How many stations can you get on that thing?"

Wow! I quickly regretted the question because the color in her face deepened to match her hair tint. Suddenly she looked like she had an itch in a place where she couldn't scratch. It really bothered me when she yelled, "How dare you…!" (expletives deleted) in a loud, indignant voice. I was immediately embarrassed and began backing away. And when all of the other shoppers turned to stare, I made sure they saw that my hands were in my pockets, and that they'd been there for a long time.

Outside in the parking lot, I peered out from behind a truck full of watermelons and watched carefully as Mz. Maven unloaded her supplies from the store pushcart, and placed them in her pickup truck beside a chainsaw. As she drove off, I noticed she had a bumper sticker that read: "Practice Beauty and Random Acts of Pleasure."

Back at home, I stared blankly and munched on saltine crackers while the Broncos beat the Cowboys by three points. I've decided to stay in more. f

68

What is it about body piercings? Those things hanging out look painful to me. Maybe the younger generation feels a need to express themselves. Why don't they try writing instead? And tattoos! I read that it's fashionable for girls to have them under their clothes. Please tell me why anyone would want a tattoo where no one can see it.

MY TWO SENSE
2 AUG
2017

THE UNFORTUNATE HICCUP

FORREST
MY TWO SENSE

In the 1940s, spectators could walk alongside golfers, even in major tournaments like the Masters. I was following Sam Snead one time when we came to his ball in the fairway. There was a rise in front of him so he turned to me and asked, "Where's the hole?" to which I replied, "I don't know." He said, "I don't either," and turned back to hit a long wood that ended up near the green. Sam won 82 professional golf tournaments, more than any other golfer in history.

While walking around my office, I paused to look at this thing. It's a hip-pocket flask that was made to hold a "3/16th pint" of libation. It says so right there on the bottom. The silver overlay on the bottle is applied by a complex chemical procedure. If it was a Russian icon, you'd have to call it an oklad, but this is different.

The swirly engraved initials near the bottom were adeptly applied, identifying an owner who will always remain a mystery to me because I can't read the fancy letters.

At the 1949 Master's Golf Tournament, I observed a nattily dressed gentleman use a pair of binoculars to watch Sam Snead putt on the 10th green. It seemed a little strange because the man was standing less than 30 feet away from where the putt was about to be attempted.

And then I noticed something else. The fan wasn't watching golf at all. He was holding a flask in his hands that looked like binoculars, and every time he raised it to his eyes, he took a swig. It was a subterfuge that very effectively disguised his odd drinking technique, and no one seemed to notice but me. Just as Sam drew his putter back to make the stroke, the natty guy hiccupped, causing the putt to jerk left a few inches and roll unceremoniously past the hole. I felt partially to blame because I just stood there and did nothing.

As the crowd moved to the next tee, the binocular guy was noticeably teetering to the starboard side. That's why I moved to the 13th fairway and watched Jimmy Demaret hit his mashie niblick shot to the green. Sam won the tournament anyway though, so I went home happy.

Surely it won't be long before our government enacts legislation that prohibits anyone from drinking and watching golf at the same time. | f

71

IN A TUCK

73

In 1952, my buddy Sammy Myers and I were stationed in Greenville, South Carolina, as buck sergeants in the Air Force. Our job was repairing airborne radars and flying radio operators on C-82s and C-119s.

Sammy and I enjoyed competing with each other on a friendly level. Compared to him, I was shorter, lighter, less gregarious, and somewhat athletically disadvantaged. But I had the instincts of jaguar, and he didn't. Maybe that gave me a slight edge in areas where results could easily be measured.

One such place was The Tower. (I hated that thing with a dedicated cynical fervor.) I don't want to think about how high it was above the lake but it was enough high for me. I had jumped off the Leon River Bridge back home in Texas a few times and it must have been about the same fall time to the water. I never heard of anyone going head first off of either one.

Sammy and I dove off the intermediate level of The Tower a few times, and jumped off the top a couple. I saw him make a nice swan dive from high up that barely caused a ripple in the water. His nonchalance made it look routine, but I knew it wasn't.

"Do a 'show off' from the top and I'll take your picture," Sam dared.

I just stared.

I'd done a few 1½ forward somersaults from a ten-foot springboard, but I didn't do them very well. My smile was a misnomer and the idea, a 1½ from the top of the tower, was certainly at odds with reality… but I was drawn to the seductive glamour of Sam's camera.

With a giant spring, I left the platform and went into a tuck that opened too late. That caused me to over-rotate and I landed on my back with a volcanic splash. The blistering pain was almost visible and my embarrassment rang out in exaggerated decibels. I kicked to the surface gasping.

"Got it," Sam yelled, "They heard the explosion in Memphis! You almost made it buddy. Try it again. I have one more shot on the roll."

Back to The Tower I went, and with all the guts I could muster, there I stood with my toes on the edge of the top platform. But this time I was mad… mad that he'd ask me to do it again after I'd just about killed myself a few minutes before.

What if I stayed in the tuck a little longer this time and went for a 2½? It was a fool's folly idea, but I wanted to show him, and his precious "one last shot on the roll."

With the knowledge that talent has no loyalty, I left the platform in a tighter tuck than before, thinking that I wanted to see the sky twice as I rotated, then quickly open and enter the water.

To my great amazement and satisfaction, that's exactly what happened. The dive was not very picturesque, but it was there, and both my body and ego were intact.

Sam got the picture, and congratulated me with a sincerity that felt really good. I never climbed the ladder on that tower again, and I don't plan to. **f**

74

Sammy and I joined the Air Force together on the 6th of September, 1950. He got out of the military after four years and went on to manage a couple of 7-11 stores in Los Angeles. His child drowned in a swimming pool, and Sammy later died of a heart attack. Some things are really hard to explain.

Late one Friday afternoon in 1951, I found myself in Eunice, Louisiana, visiting Peggy Proctor and her family for the weekend. It was raining when a buddy of mine kindly dropped me off on his way to somewhere else. Peggy and I had been dating since our early grades in high school and everyone considered me part of her clan.

At the time, I was a private first class (PFC) in the Air Force making only $95 a month, and was attending the Radar Mechanics School in Biloxi, Mississippi. I was on the red-eye shift, 6:00 to midnight.

Sunday evening came too early and I had to be back in school the next afternoon or really bad things would happen to me. The Korean War was new and the military was unreasonable about discipline. PFCs like me were easy targets.

I said my goodbyes to Peggy and told her not worry about me. When I heard her front door reluctantly close behind me, it was dark and raining, I was alone, and Biloxi was more than 200 miles away. And worse, I didn't know what the bus fare was going to cost, but I was pretty sure I didn't have nearly enough.

I held my little suitcase over my head as a defense against the constant drizzle, and started walking toward the bus station. As I walked, I heard voices coming from a little church just ahead. The front doors were open and the incandescent lights were warm and compelling. When I stepped in, two ladies saw me dripping and rushed over. With typical Cajun hospitality, they offered me coffee and a cookie.

76

RAINY NIGHT BLESSINGS

The congregation was playing Bingo. All of a sudden I was in a completely different world. I didn't have enough coins to jingle, but I did have a quarter, just one, and the sign on the wall read, "Cards – 25 Cents".

"What the heck," I thought, and I invested all of my cash. There were three winners in the first game and I was one of them. Now I had $3.75, and hope of getting back to the base was flickering.

The bus station was three blocks away and I started running. The drizzle had stopped bothering me, but when the ticket man told me the fare to Biloxi was $3.95, I went numb. I spread my $3.75 on the counter and asked if I could please buy a ticket with that amount. He knew I had to get back to my base.

While pointing with his finger, he started counting out loud, and with each word he spoke, my pulse rate quickened. "No, you can't buy a ticket with that amount," he said, and as my heart sank, he looked hard at me for another moment, "…but I'll give you the 20 cents."

I breathed a sigh of relief and waved goodbye to my new friend as I climbed into the bus. He was smiling back at me and I knew everything would be alright. ꞙ

I came away from that experience
with some thoughts to live by:

There is no such thing as a self-made man.
Never give up hope, never, never.
Don't underestimate the power of a quarter.
Look for ways to give some of it back.

78

MY TWO SENSE

FORREST
MAY
1951

The Korean War started in June, 1950, and soon afterward it was common to see young GIs walking down the street. The American people were sympathetic, so it was easy for a man in uniform to hitch a ride. Today you never see military personnel standing out beside a road with their thumbs out. Attitudes toward service men and women have changed, and not for the better.

THE QUAHADA CHIEF
ON A BLACK PONY

I was born and raised in Central Texas, where the Comanche Indians often ranged and plundered. Being an early student of their history, and an avid collector of their clothing, weapons, and photographs, my imagination long ago fell prey to their way of life. Historians call them the "Lords of the Plains," and that name is well-merited because no other tribe could sit on a horse and ride in such a handsome manner.

Of special interest to me is the Quahada band, and Quanah Parker especially. His father was Peta Nakona, chief of the Quahadas, and his mother was Cynthia Ann Parker, a white woman who, in 1836, was captured by the Comanches. She lived with them for 24 years and had three children. When she was "rescued" by Sul Ross, a Texas Ranger, and returned to her people, Cynthia Ann couldn't speak the English language anymore. She yearned to go back; a plea that was repeatedly denied. After a few years she stopped eating and died. The doctors said it was influenza.

Captain R. G. Carter

On October 10th, 1871, during the Battle of Blanco Canyon, Quanah Parker rode up to Trooper Gregg of the 4th U.S. Cavalry and shot him with a Smith & Wesson American. The trooper was interred where he fell and rocks were placed on his grave.

Captain R. G. Carter, a witness to the event, said Gregg's horse was faltering, and gave this written account:

A large and powerfully built chief led the bunch, on a coal-black racing pony. Leaning forward upon his mane, his heels nervously working in the animal's side, with six-shooter poised in air, he seemed the incarnation of savage brutal joy. His face was smeared with black war paint, which gave his features a satanic look. A large, cruel mouth added to his ferocious appearance. A full-length headdress or war bonnet of eagle's feathers, spreading out as he rode, and descending from his forehead, overhead and back, to his pony's tail, almost swept the ground. Large brass hoops were in his ears; he was naked to his waist, wearing simply leggings, moccasins and a breechclout. A necklace of bear's claws hung about his neck. His scalp lock was carefully braided in with otter fur, and tied with bright red flannel. His horse's bridle was profusely ornamented with bits of silver, and red flannel was also braided in his mane and tail, but, being black, he was not painted. Bells jingled as he rode at headlong speed, followed by the leading warriors, all eager to outstrip him in the race. It was Quanah, principal war chief of the wild Qua-ha-das.

82

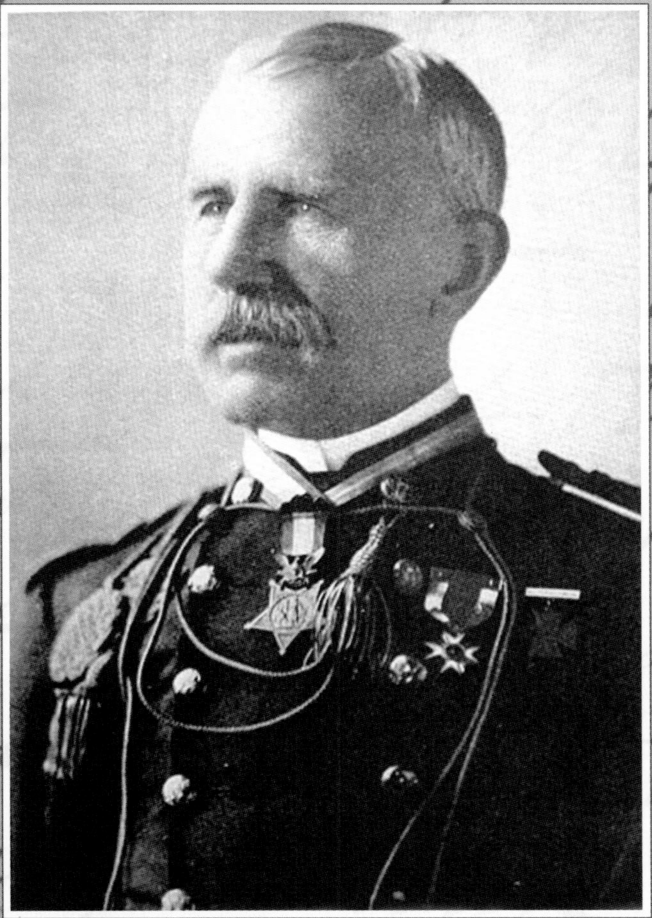

Captain Carter, who was awarded the Medal of Honor for his action in the fight, drew a map of the battle which loosely identified Gregg's burial location. Ninety-five years later, I was stationed in Lubbock, Texas, and a friend by the name of Bill Griggs and I searched relentlessly for the trooper's grave. The evidence showed it to be somewhere about 46 miles north of where I lived.

With Captain Carter's original map in hand (I didn't want to carry a copy), Bill and I hiked on weekends. Back and forth across the grassy rises and rugged dips we walked, binoculars in hand. We were ever watchful for the errant pile of rocks that were deliberately placed to keep scavenging animals from digging.

Twenty days or more we did that, often finding remnants of the fight, a canteen, a rusty knife, a brass cavalry uniform button, lots of bullet casings, but no pile of rocks. We replaced everything as it lay, lest we betray the sanctity of that battle ground.

We didn't locate Trooper Gregg's resting place. My wish now is that the chaparral and long-living creosote bushes will protect that soldier and permit him to rest in the dignity of the North Texas soil, where Mother Wind will forever wail the long mournful sound of Taps.

My motive for searching was important to me. I just wanted to stand there and render one last salute to the fallen fighter, and to "watch" as hundreds of yelping Natives and Army troopers fought one of the most decisive battles of the Indian Wars. I would like to have thrown a rock at Quanah as he sped by on his "coal-black racing pony." Hopefully I would have missed him.

84

Please allow me to explain something.

I would like to have known R.G. Carter, but he died when I was five years old. I collected his personal papers, letters, documents, and books, so I probably have more information about him than anyone alive today.

Now, about Quanah Parker: J. Evetts Haley and I went to the spot in the Palo Duro Canyon where, in 1874, General Mackenzie routed the Comanches, including Quanah. Visiting Quanah's gravesite at the Fort Sill Indian Cemetery where he's buried beside his mother and daughter (Prairie Flower), was a spiritual experience for me. I just love the Indian history of this country. f

MY TWO SENSE

Quanah went from being a ferocious Indian warrior to a statesman and leader of the Native American Church (Peyote Religion). He said, "The White Man goes into his church house and talks about Jesus, but the Indian goes into his tipi and talks to Jesus."

PRINCE OF THE COMANCHEROS

87

They say that Jose Tafoya was seven feet tall and that he stuck out of both ends of his blanket. Maybe he couldn't decide which end he wanted to keep warm. I don't know about all that, but I do know that in the 1860s and 70s, he struck a pretty wide swath through Eastern New Mexico and across the Staked Plains of North Texas.

From south of Lubbock to north of Amarillo and into Oklahoma, the land was table-flat and almost totally devoid of trees. You may be able to guess how the little town of Plainview, Texas got its name. The women who travelled the long miles across that brushless country on horseback were frequently embarrassed to the point of mortification because there was no bush to hide behind, but the men probably didn't care.

That was Indian country, and the Comanches under Chief Quanah Parker were raiding and plundering with resolve. Jose wasn't afraid. He traded the Indians cattle, horses, rifles, ammo, whisky, and anything else he could steal.

President Grant got fed up with the frequent attacks, and the order came down, "Control the Indians no matter what you have to do."

Quanah Parker

In September of 1874, General Ranald S. Mackenzie and his 4th U.S. Calvary went looking for Quanah and couldn't find him. So they tied Jose Tafoya to a wagon wheel and tortured him until he revealed that the Comanches were camped in Palo Duro Canyon. With that knowledge, the soldiers swept into the canyon, routed the Indians, burned their lodges, and killed 2,000 horses. With winter coming, and their stores gone, the 1,500 Comanches were forced to seek shelter under Army supervision at Fort Sill.

Quanah was mad at his old friend. "If I ever catch Jose Tafoya I'll boil him in oil," he warned. With that in his mind, the big Comanchero, his wife, and four children retired to his sheep ranch in New Mexico where he died in 1913.

The life or death of a Comanchero on the Staked Plains in those days often hung on the whim of a trigger finger. Rarely is it written in the annals of Western history that someone like Jose would live to be 83 years old.

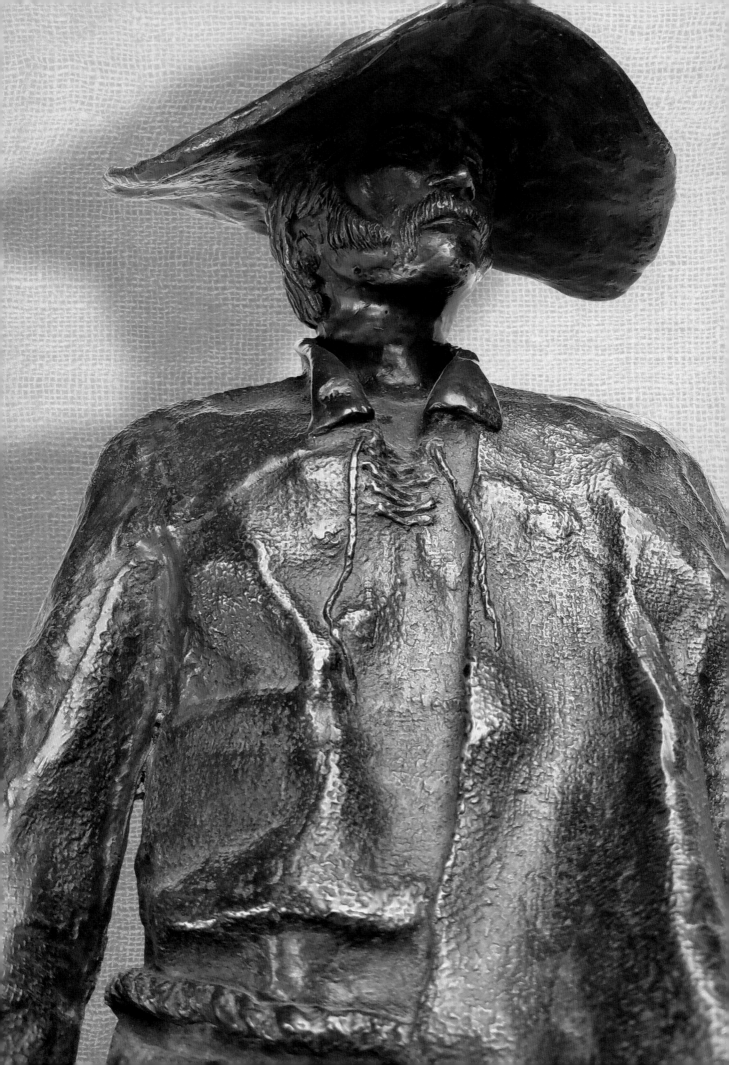

A PERSONAL SIDENOTE

Back in 1969, I was still in the Air Force and had set up a small foundry in an old abandoned grain elevator in Lubbock, Texas. I was about to cast this 28-inch portrait of Jose Tafoya, while the artist, Bill McClure, watched me put the finishing touches on the wax model. "I'm not happy with his shirt," he said. So I soaked an old piece of potato-sack burlap in hot wax, and with thick rubber gloves, I draped it around Jose's shoulders.

Bill was laughing at me.

When I poured the piece in bronze, every detail in the burlap came out perfectly, and gave us the effect we were looking for. Bill was pleased and agreed that I should be credited as co-artist.

Bill and I sold that bronze and made a few bucks that were badly needed. More than twenty years later, I was happy to buy it back from the man I sold it to. Being a pioneer is really fun. f

91

The Comancheros existed somewhere in the no-man's-land between Indians fighting soldiers, and soldiers fighting Indians. Quite often they were on both sides, which made their lives tenuous. Jose Tafoya retired, he said, because he ran out of places to hide.

MY TWO SENSE
16 SEP 196

Avalanche Lake

MONTANA GOLDEN

93

Avalanche Lake was a fairy-tale spot for me in the 1940s when I was young and could do anything. It was a few miles north and west of where, in 1959, a mountain fell and dammed the Madison River that formed Quake Lake.

To reach Avalanche Lake I had to climb about 3,000 feet over a six-mile stretch. In one spot, the trail was only 4 feet wide and had a 700-foot tumbledown drop on the left. It was a scary place and if my hat blew off, I'd never see that thing again. The Forest Service said no one ever went up there because the hike was too tough.

My father warned that grizzlies ranged in the area where I was going, so I planned to carry a dead fish. If I met a bear I'd throw the fish at him and run downhill. A grizzly's front legs are shorter than its hind legs, so I would have the advantage if it came to a race. Besides, my incentive would be greater than his.

After seven hours, I reached the lake and started fishing. The water was deep and crystal blue. Several dozen huge golden trout slowly swished through the glassy water. To my disappointment, none of them wanted any fly in my vast repertoire of lures – not even a wooly worm.

One of my most humbling dreads, and one that's most idiosyncratic of my personality, is to be ignored by a beautiful fish. I didn't catch any… not even one to throw at a griz if I met him on the down trail.

The next day, while preparing to leave, I placed my Dr. Pepper under a rock in the lake to save for next time. No need to haul it out. ZOWEE!!! That's when I noticed the freshwater shrimp. It looked like a hundred of them scurrying about. They were small, maybe a quarter-inch long, and their yellowish-translucent color made them almost invisible. That had to be the answer. That's what the fish were feeding on. I could hardly wait to get home and make some flies that imitated the shrimp.

Several weeks later, I took my old friend Donnie with me to the lake. I wanted to apply my fishing genius and show those rude trout who was their better. f

LAST LAMENT
Oh, somewhere near a placid mountain meadow,
A mariposa lily blooms its yellow best.
And on the hills and in the valleys mellow,
The chirpy plover gathers grasses for her nest.
But on a lake that tries the sportsman's skill,
He went to cast his line and catch a trout,
Alone he stood to test the wily fishes will.
And again the mighty fisherman struck out.

MY TWO SENSE

My wife and I once went on a fishing trip to Avalanche Lake. The fishing was awful and she hated when her horse jumped over trees that had fallen across the trail. The circle fire I built around her sleeping bag the first night was supposed to keep her warm (it didn't), but the "terrible" smoke kept the mosquitos at bay. The second night there was no smoke, but every time she slapped a mosquito, all of its relatives came to the funeral. There wasn't a third night.

mammoth tooth

REMNANTS OF THE PAST

Mammoths once roamed all over the Americas and if you get way out into the countryside, you might find the remnants of one. That's exactly what I did while visiting with Sam at his ranch in northeastern New Mexico back in the mid 1980's. We were far from any road when I found a 30-pound mammoth tooth. It was just lying there in plain sight. The wear patterns told us that it had belonged to a very old animal.

A mile or so farther, as we walked along a barely flowing stream of water, I discovered a tusk. It had been exposed to the elements for a long time because the ivory had dried and layers were popping off in fragments. I guessed it was a mammoth because mastodons are not commonly found in the Southwest, and their tusks were a different shape.

I started excavating in the cement-like clay that engulfed the tusk. The bursitis-inducing work progressed slowly with a small handpick.

Meanwhile Sam scavenged the surrounding area, searching for artifacts. Suddenly, he discovered a knife eroding from the bank of the stream. It was about three inches long and was made of Edwards Plateau flint. Heavy-use damage on both blade edges indicated that it had probably been used to cut bone. We knew that tool could not be associated with the mammoth because the flake patterns were not Clovis technology.

I continued working as the sun burned low in the sky. Finally, about two hours later, the tusk was completely uncovered.

My efforts to learn when the mammoth died proved futile because there wasn't enough collagen left in the ivory to obtain a carbon-14 date. That meant the animal died in very ancient times – perhaps 50,000 years ago or more.

The mammoth tusk weighed 70 pounds when I got it to my house. Over the years it has dried and crumbled into a sad likeness of what it used to be, and I have given big pieces of it to friends and museums.

I always intended to go back to Sam's ranch and dig out the mammoth's skull and other tusk, but now, at age 87, I know that won't happen. I wonder what that softly flowing stream will look like when my bones don't have enough collagen in them to carbon date. |f

There is an inherent thrill in finding a paleo projectile, and I've done so only a few times. In 1954, near Schertz, Texas, I found an Angostura point that was made from Edwards Plateau Chert. It was meant to kill a mammoth, and I knew that no one had set eyes on it for 9,000 years or more. I was reluctant to touch it and bring it into the 20th century, but after a few minutes of reverence, I picked it up.

MY TWO SENSE

THINGS I COVET

I used to collect paint palettes. I had about 20 of those things and they looked so good hanging on a wall in our guest house, that when we sold the business I just left them there (except for a couple of course).

Clark Hulings gave this one to me. He was a special friend whose work was sold in our gallery. Clark was getting a lot of publicity and winning awards at important shows, so his work quickly escalated in value. In the early 1970s, I gave my wife one of his paintings for her birthday. I paid $6,500 for it.

After a few years, Peggy's mother retired. She had been managing a ladies' ready-to-wear store in San Angelo, Texas. My wife came to me and said, "You know, Honey, I really love that Hulings painting you gave me, but my mother needs a place to live and I'd like to help her." The painting had doubled in value more than a few times, so we sold it and bought Peggy's mother a nice home with the money.

Clark Hulings

I still have one small floral by Clark. It's called *A Single Rose*. My wife thinks it's hers and I don't have the guts to tell her it isn't. Does that mean it's hers? Wish I'd kept some of his larger works.

Ben Stahl was another friend. He was the kind of guy you wanted to be around and stay around. We had a show for him, and one of the most popular paintings depicted a cowboy on a ladder who was about to climb into a hay loft. The title was *The Way the West was Won*. We sold it quickly and could've sold it another ten times over. Ben painted this condensed version and gave it to me.

One of Ben's favorite subjects was saloon scenes. They had combustion and usually included ladies who were familiar with the nighttime jingle of spurs.

Both Clark and Ben painted subjects that made me feel warm and comfortable. There aren't many artists around today that have that same flavor. f

MY TWO SENSE

Ben Stahl illustrated the novels "Gone with the Wind" and "Little Women", and had more than 750 of his paintings featured in The Saturday Evening Post.

Ben Stahl

Moses was an important figure in the Bible. I wonder why more male babies today are not named Moses.

As I watched Leo Salazar carve this 24-inch figure from a freshly cut tree, he assured me that it would be a perfect likeness of Moses and I believed him. Who else would throw his arms out like that except to summon the Israelites and lead them out of Egypt and across the Red Sea to Mount Sinai?

"That's where Moses received the Ten Commandments," Leo said, as he spoke like some kind of omniscient religious guru. His words were fit for lessons at any Sunday school.

It was interesting to watch his sharp knife skillfully whittle the wood, which did little to resist the artist's efforts. As the face of Moses began to appear, Leo's smile brightened. I just sat there and grinned.

Several hours later, there stood the prophet in his majestic flowing robe. I gave $350 for the beautiful figure just because I enjoyed Leo so much. But Moses had been an old man, and this portrait looked too white and new. I solved the problem by standing him on the balcony of my house so the sun and snow could act as aging agents.

After about three years the wind toppled Moses over and broke his right hand. I glued it back on and stood him up again, where he stayed for another three years. Finally, Moses took on the weathered personality I thought he deserved.

Moses now stands in my home on the second step that leads into my den, and his expression continues to telegraph a timeless message. As I type the final words to this story, I glance over and see him looking at me. I like my Moses. f

SALUTE TO A WARRIOR

When Renelle Jacobson stepped out of her car in my driveway, and walked toward me, I was charmed at first sight. Her smile telegraphed a cautionary message: "Look out world, because here I come." She had read about my hidden treasure in *Hemispheres*, the in-flight magazine for United Airlines, and said to me, "I ripped out the pages, stuffed them in my bag, and told the passenger sitting next to me, 'Oh, I am SO going to find this when I get home.'"

With a treasure-hunting partner, she soon hit the road for Yellowstone. "I was bouncing off the walls with an overload of excitement. This adventure is for every little girl and boy who have desperately wanted to look for a hidden treasure. I know I'm silly, but some of us are lucky enough to never completely grow up." She returned from that first road trip empty-handed but, "We had a blast. I've since gone back three or four times."

However, there is one small problem; Renelle, 41 and single, has a rare bone cancer called osteosarcoma. A few years of chemo and several surgeries didn't kill the disease, so in 2011, her left leg was amputated above the knee. She has a prosthetic leg but the ongoing cancer changes her limb shape. "Sometimes I can walk quite well and sometimes I can't."

A friend loaded her in his Bell helicopter and they searched the far reaches of Yellowstone Park.

"We discovered some top secret waterfalls — at least that's how I romanticized them in my mind. They were out in the middle of nowhere."

"We also flew over Hebgen Lake and had lunch in West Yellowstone. What a grand day for a cancer patient who is trapped inside most of the time."

Renelle, whose constitution is made of sinew-tough fiber, is now in her 5th year of chemotherapy. With an expression that reflected her longing, she said to me, "I'm sick three or four days a week, have low energy the rest of the time, and my sleep schedule is often turned upside down. Working on this treasure hunt has given me a way to occupy my time when I'm awake after midnight. When I work on your puzzle for an hour, I can say that I worked toward a goal." She added, with a voice as soft as her eyes, "I'll keep working on the poem every night until the moment when I can call my hunting buddies and say, 'Let's hit the road.'" Imagination is her pleasure and faith is her nourishment.

Renelle Jacobson inspires me in a singular way; her spirit holds me in thrall. Each day she tests the extremes in ways I can't even imagine. To know her even a little bit, as I do, is to love her a lot.

TO PARAPHRASE CHARLOTTE BRONTE:

"Her human heart has hidden treasures,
In secret kept, in silence sealed;
The thoughts, the hopes, the dreams, the pleasures,
Whose charms enrapture when revealed"

POSTSCRIPT

Too soon after this story was written Renelle fell victim to the terrible disease that had consumed her body. She lived alone, and in one of her last emails to me she expressed concern for her horse. When the world learned that Renelle had passed away the angels cried and I lowered my heart to half-mast. f

Hebgen Lake

Renelle had crutches that were upholstered with beautiful cobalt blue cloth. Her mom made them for her, and each one had pockets that held something Renelle needed: glasses, wallet, lipstick, cell phone, comb – you name it. When someone saw her coming they smiled, and she smiled back. It was contagious.

110

THE IRON ROOSTER OF SANTA FE COUNTY

Google them and look at their paintings. James Asher and Joe Anna Arnett, Santa Fe

Years ago, I got a bargain on two old cast iron chickens. They're probably 20th-century Spanish, or from over there someplace. The rooster weighs 70 pounds and is almost two feet tall, and here's a photo of the old hen. Both were rusty brown and ugly-dull finished, especially the rooster.

I really liked those antique things, but when my wife saw them on our kitchen table, she asked if I was okay and felt my forehead to see if I had a temperature. That suddenly gave me terrible buyer's remorse. I looked at those chickens again, and out into the garage they went. It really bothers me to make bad art decisions like that, but then I thought of my friend Joe Anna Arnett.

No one in the world is better at painting still life florals than she is, and it's impossible not to love her. That's an envious position for anyone to be in.

One call to my old friend brought her running with her husband, Jim Asher, who also is a world-class artist. I thought if anyone could put paint on that rooster and make it look good, it'd be Joe Anna.

She took one look at it and groped for the nearest chair. I'm sure she was thinking, "Oh my, what did I do to deserve this?" She had never put paint on a piece of iron before, at least not a cold and heavy, tall, brown one. She was not smiling when I put that thing in the back of her car. At home, Jim put it by a heater to warm it up, probably hoping it would melt.

I didn't hear from Joe Anna for a month, and then one day an email came in. She wanted to bring my chicken back. I just knew she was weary of it, and whatever catastrophes that occurred in her studio would probably be my fault. Maybe it fell over and broke her paint box, or the weight of it collapsed a leg on her Woodbridge table and sent her coffee cup splashing across the floor. I didn't feel too good about it.

The iron rooster was covered with a black garbage bag when Jim put it on my kitchen table and then stepped back behind the counter. I looked at Joe Anna and she looked at me, neither of us smiling. After a long few seconds, she nodded toward the plastic bag, indicating that I should pull it off.

Wow, this is what was under the bag. When Joe Anna saw me grinning she started laughing, and we hugged. I love it when I make really great art decisions like that. |f

112

Someday Joe Anna's paintings will show at the Metropolitan Museum in New York.

MY TWO SENSE
14 OCT
1953

LESSONS FROM FORREST

There was this really good potter I used to know back in Lubbock, Texas. Forrest Gist was his name, or maybe it was Forest Gist, I don't remember which, so I'll call him Forrest because I like that name better.

I had purchased one of his bowls from a store and gave it to my wife for her birthday. She liked it so much I thought it might be nice to get her another one for Christmas.

So I went to see Forrest when I knew he'd be firing about 30 pottery vessels in a large outdoor kiln. I arrived just in time to see him remove a smoldering hot jar with a stick, look at it for a few seconds, and then throw it on the cement sidewalk where it splattered. What the…?

I approached Forrest cautiously, not completely cognizant of his mind-set, and was careful to remember that he had a hot stick in his hand. "Whatcha doin', Forrest?" I asked respectfully. He didn't answer, but instead, threw another hot jar on the pavement. This went on a couple more times before I decided to be rude to my friend.

"What are you, crazy? I'll buy some of those things from you!" He turned to me and politely said,

FORREST
FENN
MAJOR USAF

117

"Look Forrest, I'm experimenting with a new glaze here. I want quality to be my signature, and if these pieces don't measure up to my standards then I don't want my name on them." Gee, and I thought they were really good.

I helped Forrest clean up the mess caused by the demise of one kiln's-worth of fired clay "junkers," and I had to admit that this was a master artist at work. Although I didn't agree completely with his quality control methods, I respected his philosophy.

What I'd seen Forrest do preyed on my mind for the next several days. I had already decided to be a world-class bronze sculptor, and was sure that my first two efforts into the art world had served as excellent platforms from which to launch my career.

Technically speaking, what I lacked in talent could be compensated for in other ways. For instance, when I couldn't get the hooves on my buffalo just right, I solved the problem by having him stand in the mud. And my *Self-Portrait as Pilot*, well, surely my skill would improve over time… maybe over a long time.

Going to Forrest Gist's pot firing and seeing how he suffered through his craft ruined my promising art career, so I decided to be an art dealer instead. The two bronzes remain in my collection to remind me never to try that again. f

MY TWO SENSE

On May 2, 2002, the 4th version of "The Scream" by Edvard Munch, came on the block at Sotheby's Auction House in London. I thought it was a terrible painting until it sold for $119,922,600. Maybe that says something about my knowledge of art, and my taste.

MEMORIES THAT NEVER DIE

They don't build guys like George Dabich anymore. If you saw him walking down the street wearing a brown cowboy hat you probably wouldn't be impressed. He wasn't tall, athletic, flashy, famous, or rich. But you'd run out of things he "wasn't" pretty fast, because he had assets we all should wish to emulate.

As a 22-year-old sailor in World War II, George was cruising the South Pacific on a destroyer, the USS *Brooks*, when it was hit by a kamikaze. George was blasted end-over-end out into the ocean where he flailed around in burning oil and gasoline for hours, until he was rescued and brought aboard another destroyer, the USS *Hovey*. Less than 24 hours later, the *Hovey* was torpedoed and sank, and once again George was left thrashing in the burning ocean.

After the Navy, George settled in Cody, Wyoming, where he became a professional outbacker and hunting guide. He also took up oil painting and started making some pretty good Indian pictures.

When we met back in 1967, I was training pilots in the Air Force, but had orders to Vietnam. His parting words to me were, "If you come back whole, I'll take you out where we can pick up some buffalo caps and maybe a skull or two." We were both collecting Western history things, and that invitation may have motivated me to fly faster and keep my head down deeper.

Upon my return, I set up an art foundry in my garage, and gave George a hunk of wax so he could create some figures for me to cast in bronze. From there, our relationship flourished and we became close friends.

George kept his promise and took me out into the Skylight country north of Cody, where we found a half-dozen buffalo horn caps and a few skulls.

This young bull is my best one. It was covered with reddish-yellow lichen, the faded remnants of which can still be seen between the horns and down. I removed the pine needles that populated the eye sockets and nose cavity.

A basalt arrowhead is imbedded in the bone just inside the bull's left eye. It penetrated only half an inch, and broke where it was affixed to the arrow shaft. It didn't kill the animal, however, and the bone healed around the stone point, holding it tight. I wish it had been me with the Indian who released that arrow to fly its last mission.

The brown hat I wear so proudly was George's. He wore it while his hunters killed 28 grizzlies out there just east of Yellowstone. He placed it on my head beside a campfire one night, and said, "Fits you like a glass fits water, so I want you to have it."

George died at age 91, and his passage went largely unnoticed save for a scant few guys like me and some relatives. But the coyotes and

basalt arrowhead

sagebrush know he's gone, and so do the tall pines, under which he sat so many times and drank coffee from a tin cup. The red embers of his campfires will miss him badly, but not as much as me. **f**

"In my solitude, it haunts me with memories of days gone by. In my solitude, it taunts me, with reveries that never die."

Thank you, Tony Bennett.

MY TWO SENSE

I recall times when I've eaten too much chocolate, and some may say I've written too much about George Dabich. I'm not sorry for doing either of those things, although I fail to see a correlation between the two.

ME AND MUMMY JOE

Only a few minutes after leaving the East Entrance of Yellowstone, on the way to Cody, Wyoming, you'll see a big cave off to the left if you're paying attention. Its mouth is 150-feet-wide and looks like a giant opera singer yawning in the side of the mountain. The beautiful North Fork of the Shoshoni River splashes the opposite side of the road right there.

The cave didn't have a name when I first knew it, but it always made a strong impression on me. It was a favorite lunchtime respite for

125

my family whenever we headed back to Texas after a summer in Yellowstone. I usually climbed into the cave and sat on a rock in the back to eat Fritos and drink my Dr. Pepper. That was in the 1930s and '40s.

Twenty-five years later, I became friends with two of the men who excavated the cave in the 1960s. They were Bob Edgar and George Dabich. For two years they carefully moved rocks, shoveled dirt, screened for artifacts, compiled data, and helped uncover Mummy Joe.

That's how Mummy Cave finally got its name.

Once, when George and I were having dinner at the Erma Café in Cody, he spoke of watching an archaeologist uncover an Angostura

MADE BY GEORGE DABICH
FROM MOUNTAIN SHEEP BONE FROM
"MUMMY CAVE" NEAR CODY WYO.
FOUND IN THE 3RD LAYER.
682 AD (± 100 YRS.)

FORREST FENN 1967

point that was 28 feet below the cave's surface. The weapon had been flaked to kill an ancient species of bison and had not seen daylight for almost 9,000 years.

George also talked about the artifacts he had uncovered: stone choppers, hammers and grinders, projectile points, cordage, fragments of tanned sheepskin, broken arrow shafts, basketry, rabbit nets, and more than 2,000 leftover animal bones that had been discarded by the ancient dwellers.

In 1967, I received a gift from George. It was a five-inch-long knife he'd carved from a mountain sheep bone that came from layer #3. He said it carbon-14 dated to about 682 AD.

George's tales were colorful and compelling. He spoke of what it was like living in the cave 1,200 years ago when Mummy Joe died, and of the trail-weary hunters who returned from a hunt dragging elk hides full of meat that would sustain their clans through the freezing-cold winters. I was fascinated by the stories.

After midnight, with George's words fresh on my mind, I drove to Mummy Cave. The night was so black that even the snow-covered ground offered little moderation. With a small light as my only companion, I climbed up and in, and sat on my old rock against the back wall. In the lonely silence, nothing moved but the wind, whispering its way through the trees, down the river, and past the cave.

As I sat in the eerie silence, I could feel the austere grandeur of my surroundings. Who were these ancient people who called this cave home? Over the last few thousand years, several hundred nature-

126

127

toughened Indians had rested their butts on the very rock upon which I sat. I just knew it. Can you imagine how that made me feel?

Today my thoughts sometimes hearken back to Mummy Joe, who was wrapped in sheepskins so long ago and buried deep in the dirt. What would I have thought when I was a kid, sitting on my rock, knowing that Joe was just a few feet away? Are there any among you who are as intrigued by America's ancient past as I am? Tell me. f

MY 2 SENSE

I wonder about the lives that were lost during our world wars. Most of the people are nameless today. Millions of homes were blown up, and the rubble was later carted away. What was in that rubble? Mummy Cave is a dwelling that was occupied for at least 9,000 years. Will we someday excavate the European landfills? I hope so because I think they deserve it.

U. S. CAVALRY
TACTICS.

1841.

Y AU
AUG. 1862

CASEY'S
INFANTRY
TACTICS

VOL. III

Van Nostrand

THIS BOOK IS THE PROPERTY OF THE U. S.
FOR THE USE OF
COMPANY "a"
OF THE
"7th" U. S. CAVALRY.

It will be accounted for on the Muster Rolls of
the Company.

ALGERNON'S RELATIVE

A relation of Algernon Smith once marched into my gallery reeking of a very strong libation, and handed me three little books he was looking to sell. Slurring his words, he began telling me about the original owner, not knowing that I probably knew more about the man than he did. When he mentioned his price, which was three times too high, I grabbed my wallet before he could change his mind.

The relative strode smiling from my office rubbing his hands together. Once his new money was spent on Jim Beam, he'd have nothing to show for our deal, but I'd have these three treasures to keep forever.

HERE'S WHY THEY ARE IMPORTANT TO ME.

In 1863, Lieutenant Algernon Smith was assigned as Aide-de-Camp to Major General Alfred Terry, and that was interesting to me because 92 years and a few wars later, I too would be assigned Aide-de-Camp to a Major General.

Algernon was born in 1842 and later had an auspicious career in the Civil War. He had several horses shot from under him, and each time he toppled to the ground unhurt. He survived the fierce battle at Cold Harbor, the fight at Drury's Farm, and a few others. In 1865, he was severely wounded when he took a bullet at Fort Fisher, near the Cape Fear River.

He bounced back, and in 1867 after the war was over, Algernon found himself assigned to the 7th US Cavalry Regiment commanded by General George Armstrong Custer; a man who washed his teeth with salt, but in whose company Algernon was particularly comfortable.

For the next nine years, Custer and Smith fought side-by-side through some major Indian wars, including The Battle on the Washita in 1868 and The Yellowstone Campaign in 1873. But three years later, Mother Luck took a ferocious turn against Algernon.

It was June 25, 1876, when as Commander of Company E, Algernon rode into the Valley of the Little Bighorn River with the whole of the 7th US Cavalry. Within a few hours, 258 of those fighting men were dead, including Custer. A bullet had cleaved a tunnel through his side even as another pierced his proud breast. Algernon abandoned his men to join his commander on "Last Stand Hill," where they fell together, side-by-side. Algernon's body, riddled with arrows, lay supine upon the hard-baked ground. He was 33 years old. They both failed to hear the last brash roll of musketry as it rolled across the hot Montana sky. Fickle is the finger that points at success.

The best book on the Custer fight, *Son of the Morning Star*, was written by Evan Connell who was practically a hermit. Nevertheless, he never failed to walk down the hill from his house in Santa Fe and meet me for Coffee at the Plaza Café. Both his memory and his golden words are two treasures that I will never hide.

In one of my next lives I want to be Evan Connell. f

INSTRUCTION, EXERCISE, AND MANŒUVRES

VERNON'S RELATIVE

OF

LINE OF SKIRMISHER

BRIGADE,

SEY,

ARMÉE.

WAY.

By

A NEW SYSTEM OF SWORD EXERCISE

O'ROURKE

EVAN S. CONNELL

Son of the Morning Star

CUSTER AND
THE LITTLE BIGHORN

9-10-84

Dear Forrest—

Here is the book I have been
promising—publication date
is actually Oct 15th so you
are one of the first to have
a copy—by the way, an autograph
from Evan is a rarity —so
the value is increased.
Anyway, hope you enjoy the Custer
study—It will be getting
a lot of press in the next
month.
Again, thanks for your
hospitality!

Sincerely,

Jean

Jean Conger

Dear Forrest,
This is just off the press, though
you might enjoy it.

Best wishes,

Evan Connell

Evan Connell

Algernon Smith spent a big part of his life in the saddle, and at locations where his survival depended on the accuracy of someone else's rifle. He was a victor most of the time, but not always.

FORREST
MY TWO SENSE
10 SEP
1984

CULTURES ON TOP OF CULTURES

"When war is rife, and danger's nigh,
'God and the soldier' 's all the cry.
When the war is o'er, and the danger righted,
God is forgotten, and the soldier slighted." *

Tucker Wyche was a veteran of the ground fighting on Iwo Jima during WWII, and was left with some noticeable mental and physical scars — especially physical. His wife said that his medical needs were abandoned by his government, and I could see it was true.

The small Wyche ranch in Northern Arizona was sparse of grass, which interpolated into few cows. So Tucker found comfort in the saddle wandering through the tangled cedar brakes trying to find new-born calves ahead of the mountain lions that were constantly on the prowl.

Once, when I was riding with him, we happened by a small rock shelter that was hidden behind a knot of cottonwoods in a tight canyon. The cave-like dwelling had been inhabited in prehistoric times as was indicated by a few potsherds and lithics that were scattered around the floor.

There also was an old, Copenhagen snuff can from the 20s or 30s, I guessed. It made me wonder if Paleo Man, 10,000 years earlier, also had taken refuge in that little space.

Against the back wall was a stone-outlined hearth. I scraped in the ashes with a stick hoping to find a few recognizable animal bones that would tell me what the ancient dwellers ate. To my delight I uncovered a 5½ inch chert knife that was tightly wrapped with a stretch of sinew. It was enough to make several bow strings. The blade had heavy use-damage on both edges. I guessed that it had been stored in the dead ashes to prevent small gnawing animals from chewing on the sinew, which still looked fresh and usable.

A few short months later Tucker passed away, ostensibly from his war-related wounds, and his wife moved far away to be near their children.

A number of widely varied cultures had occupied that small shelter through some hard times, and then disappeared. Makes me wonder if the residents 100 years from now will again need sinew to make bow strings. **f**

* New Colorado and the Santa Fe Trail by Augustus Allen Hayes 1880

MY TWO SENSE

I especially liked Tucker Wyche. He enjoyed riding around his ranch with only his horse and dog for company. Even with all of his maladies, there was an aura of unruffled repose about him.

THE EVOLUTION
OF MY ART OPINION

137

My art career in Santa Fe began at a snail's stride. One problem was that more than half my life had been spent flying fighters in the Air Force, and I was an artistic lowbrow with no college or business acumen. Art was an entirely new idea for me, and I didn't own a single painting. So I borrowed a few and advertised them full-page color in the most prestigious magazines of the day, *Apollo* and *Connoisseur*. I was hoping the big collectors who didn't know me would think I was an expert.

Fortunately, we happened to be in the right place at the right time, with the right product. I say "product" because I thought an artist was a manufacturer and the painting she or he produced was a commodity. What was the difference between General Motors making a Chevrolet and Roseta Santiago making a painting? Seemed reasonable to me, but that was back in 1972.

In 1975, we acquired a nice painting by Nicolai Fechin for $7,500, and sold it two weeks later for $15,000. That was a hundred percent profit in two weeks, or 2,600% profit amortized over a year. I was liking the art business, but I still had so much to learn. I didn't know

the difference between abstract and modern art, or even if there was a difference.

> *Abstract art uses a visual language of shape, form, color, and line to create a composition which may exist with a degree of independence from visual references in the world.*
> *(This taken directly from Wikipedia.org)*

Wassily Kandinsky – Ugh! You can have that guy. I couldn't even understand the definition of what he was doing. His work found no home in my affections.

> *Modern art is usually associated with art in which the traditions of the past have been thrown aside in a spirit of experimentation.*
> *(This taken directly from Wikipedia.org)*

Well, that was a little better, but the beauty of Pablo Picasso's *Le Déjeuner sur l'Herbe* was way beyond the reach of my imagination. The look of that thing rippled over me in a way that I had not known since some guy tried to sell me an Andy Warhol painting of a tin can. I avoided dealers who dealt in that kind of art for fear they'd turn their vocabulary loose on me.

In 1988, we sold our gallery and I signed a five year no-compete clause with the new owner. That moved me away from the business,

Wassily Kandinsky

and almost immediately I went from knowing nearly everyone in the Western art scene, to not knowing anyone.

After a few years being out of the business I felt isolated and longed to get back the camaraderie that surrounds artists and what they do. So in 2007, I commissioned Roseta Santiago to paint the cover of my book *Historic American Indian Dolls*. Everyone loved it.

While I was out on the art periphery I couldn't help but notice what was happening. The Fechin painting that we sold a few years earlier for $15,000, hammered at auction for $850,000.

Over time, I learned how the manufacture of Chevrolets is different from what a painter does, and why the value of an artist's work should not be determined by the hours expended. The art world has changed so much over the last few decades, along with my understanding of it.

During the first two-thirds of the 20th century there were 80 significant male artists for every important female artist, and I couldn't understand why. But today, with so many lady painters coming into prominence, it is obvious that talent is not decided by the arrangement of chromosomes.

Today, when I walk into Santa Fe galleries like Blue Corn, Manitou, or Matteucci I am amazed at the quality of what I see. I would like to buy nearly everything that's hanging on the walls.

With the value of good art appreciating like it is today, maybe I'll start saving my money and buy another one of Roseta's paintings. **f**

"Artistic Road Kill"

Here's a piece of art that hangs in my garage. It's a fake Andy Warhol, but I like it. I picked it up in the middle of Galisteo Street a few years ago. It would probably bring a lot of money at one of the big auction houses in New York.

DOUG HYDE IN STONE

Doug and I happened upon the art scene at about the same time. That was back in 1972. His sculptures had a small, but budding following in Scottsdale, Arizona, which is where most of the money for contemporary Western art was coming from.

About 20 collectors held up that market, and if there had been an art marquee in town someplace, a few names would have been at the top of it: Eddie Basha who owned a large chain of grocery stores, Henry Topf, Kay Miller of Miller Brewing Co., and the wonderful widow, Thelma Kieckhefer.

Doug and I were a good team, and we treated those Arizona clients with adroitness and polish, the likes of which they never witnessed again. Doug made hundreds of stone sculptures, Scottsdale wanted them, and my gallery did the selling.

My wife and I liked Doug's work so much we kept two pieces for ourselves.

This alabaster lady is not tall, just two feet, but she's really heavy. That's why she has been sitting on our living room fireplace without moving for almost 30 years. I couldn't lift even half of her. She was

isolated and lonesome, but then our great-granddaughter Arden came along, and at age two, fell in love with the sculpture. That's when I named the stone pueblo woman holding a pot, *Lady Pretty Blanket.* When the house was too quiet, we'd look over there and see Arden and "Lady" sitting side-by-side talking to each other, and sometimes hugging. So of course we gave the sculpture to Arden, but she can't take possession until my wife and I are gone. Ha!

Doug Hyde is mostly Nez Perce, and he possesses bold Native features and a strong code of ethics. During the many years we worked together (mostly without contracts), there was nothing but handshakes and pleasantness.

My other Doug Hyde sculpture is 27 inches tall. It epitomizes a dignified Nez Perce chief whose name has long been forgotten. His feather fan and drop-alongside earrings are testaments to his stature

145

Alan Simpson,
Joe Medicine Crow,
Forrest Fenn

147

in his tribe. He stands facing the wall in my kitchen now because the sight reminds me of the great Henry Farny painting, *The Song of the Talking Wire*.

To me, both figures personify the West at a threshold moment when the first faint sound of change was beginning to resonate across the silent mountains. The western landscape was changing fast to make room for the "giant horse that gallops on iron rails." There's the same sadness in the painted Indian's face that I notice in Doug's sculpture. Can you see tears of sorrow building in the eyes of those two Plains warriors? I can, and I wish my inadequate words about that sentiment were more eloquent.

Joe Medicine Crow died at age 102 and was the last War Chief of the Crow Tribe. His great uncle, White Man Runs Him, was a scout for General Custer at the Battle of the Little Bighorn. Many years ago, Joe said to me in a wistful moment, "When I was just a little Indian kid running around, my elders told me about our history. I asked them if the government would ever give our future back to us." I hope so, Joe. f

MY TWO SENSE
27 OCT

When I first met Doug Hyde he was a stone sculptor, and rocks are a heavy medium. His son, Buffalo, was born with only one arm, but was more than capable of moving heavy pieces around his father's studio. Today Buffalo Hyde is no longer moving rocks, but is an internationally acclaimed painter. Google him to see his work.

APACHES IN THE GARAGE

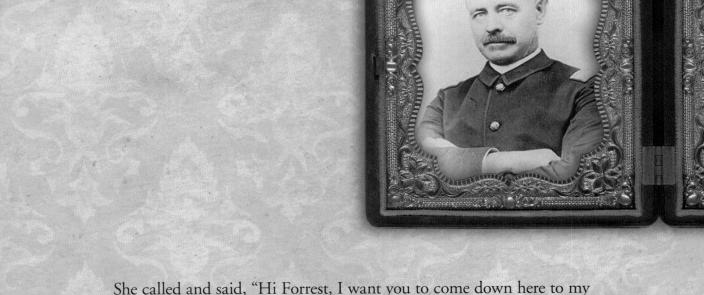

She called and said, "Hi Forrest, I want you to come down here to my garage sale." Yeah, sure. She was in San Antonio and I was in Santa Fe. I said, "Josette, wake up, you're having a nightmare. Did you really ask me to come 619 nautical miles great circle route against the wind just to attend your garage sale? What're you selling besides tamales?"

"Yes, Forrest," she said, "It's because you're such a class act and the tamales are delicious. Call me with your ETA and I'll pick you up at Stinson Field," and then she hung up.

Well, what do you say to a woman like that? I thought of her fawn-like brown eyes, and remembered they were ardent enough to attract the admiration of even the most indifferent. She was also an old friend and a no-nonsense antique dealer who had sold me some nice things in the past. Plus, she did have a "You'd better come along sonny," sound to her voice.

On the way from the airport to her warehouse, she explained that she was liquidating the estate of General John Bullis, whose distinguished career was not unknown to me. In 1886, he served with General Nelson A. Miles in his quest to capture Geronimo. Camp Bullis in San

one of the Bullis baskets

Antonio was named for him. I was suddenly so thrilled with Josette that when we stopped at McDonald's for lunch, I said she could have anything on the menu. I paid of course.

Thirty-minutes and twelve-bucks-fifty later, we were looking at the Bullis Collection. In a small box was a letter dated March 12, 1886, from the general to his wife, "We swept into a large Apache village and captured eight big ollas full of grain. I kept a nice woman's perforator bag for you." The letter was resting on the bag.

In Josette's quiet and unobtrusive way, she announced that because the sale had been advertised, she was honor-bound to hold everything until her warehouse opened at 0700 the next morning. The decision displayed the integrity that was idiosyncratic of her nature, and it gave me time to review the inventory and prices. There were Navajo blankets and jewelry, Plains Indian beaded things, two painted buffalo robes, a nice Tesuque dance kilt, some Hopi pottery, and lots of other stuff I liked.

That night, Josette prepared a wonderful meal for me and her family, and the dessert was bread pudding – my all-time favorite. At 07:01 the next morning, I handed Josette a check for the entire garage sale. She agreed to pack everything in a U-Haul and deliver it to my

150

perforator bag or awl case

John Bullis distinguished himself during the Civil War and later while fighting the Indians. He retired from the Army in 1905 with the rank of Brigadier General. Six years later, while watching a boxing match, he suffered an apoplexic stroke and died. He was 70 years old, and totally used up.

MY TWO SENSE

151

gallery in Santa Fe. I felt good because her commission was forty percent of the estate, plus expenses, and another free meal from me.

This time we dined at the Bull Ring and I hinted that she should have a burger. When she started ordering, my hopes of frugality dwindled and then vanished as my wallet slid rapidly into the dark abyss of commitment. "To start, I'll have a glass of 2005 Valandraud, St-Emilion. Wait, better make it a bottle. And for dinner I'll have the cobb salad, prime rib – make it an end-cut – with au jus and horseradish, potatoes au gratin, and sweet crepes." For dessert, she had the crème brulee, and of course, an expensive French liqueur "to freshen my palate." I had a lettuce salad and a glass of water.

That meal blew my budget pretty quick, but she was great company and did me a couple of important favors. She also helped me resell some of the things I'd bought from the estate sale, so I guess it was worth it in the end.

I have fond memories of the time with Josette, and the deals we made. She always taught me something that I needed to know. ▮f

ME AND MICHAEL DOUGLAS

Back in the early 1980's, I purchased about 200 large African sculptures from a good trader friend of mine named Sosoko. There were Dogon, Bamana, and Yoruba tribe carvings, pieces from Benin, house posts, ancestral beings, and various fertility figures.

I was still making an inventory when Michael Douglas wandered into my gallery. I had not met him before, but I knew his resume was crammed with accomplishments that would humble even the most self-possessed. He stayed in our guest house and we socialized for a short time. I was impressed with how normal and down-to-earth he was. I asked him how he avoided being overly affected by his successes, which included winning an Academy Award. His response spoke to his humanity. "Because, as Kirk Douglas' son, I grew up with all of those big-shot Hollywood stars."

Michael enjoyed antiques and wound up purchasing five of my African statues. They were large, gangly, and hard to ship, so I decided to pack them in my airplane and personally deliver them to his front door. A week later, the two of us were chewing some finger foods and drinking wine beside his pool, which overlooked all of Hollywood.

FORREST
MY TWO SENSE
6 JUN

I loved it when famous people came into our gallery. Sam Shepherd and Jessica Lange lived in Santa Fe, and would stop in sometimes. She was always a little stretched out when people didn't recognize her right away.

Between the company and the view, I was afforded a fleeting but enjoyable moment of preeminence.

After a few minutes, Michael went into his house for more wine, leaving me alone to revel in the flourish of his opulence. Just then, a man wearing a low thread-count sweater, short-shorts, slosh slippers, and rose-colored glasses entered through the gate and sat down beside me on a bench. He was also wearing a rather toothy smile. We introduced ourselves, but his name didn't register, and then we talked for a few minutes. He seemed poised and confident, but otherwise ordinary. Suddenly he glanced at his watch, mumbled something, and departed with some urgency. "How strange that was," I thought.

When Michael returned, I mentioned what had happened. He said, "Yeah," I saw him through the window. That was Elton John. He lives in the neighborhood and comes by once in a while."

When I told that story to my daughters they laughed, and reminded me of something I keep reminding myself: that I was born a hundred years too late. If it had been Billy the Kid that sat beside me on the bench, I'd have recognized him. f

IS IT MY CANDY ANN?

A beachcomber with sand between her toes
posted this object to me
and asked me what it was.
It arrived with a note — a dare —
and was thoughtful
enough to make me pause,
but too personal to share.
I hope the reader will forgive
my impassioned response to her.
My only excuse is that it's late at night.

A wanderer chanced upon this driftwood art,
Shipwrecked and lonely on a sandy shore.
At least to me it plays that part; an olden sailing ship,
And nothing more.

Or maybe it's a desperate soul,
An eager sort, standing on a woody knoll,
Waiting for the whirling Candy Ann,
Who, in her usual rescue chore,
Will come to get the willing man,
And bring him home forevermore.

Maybe it's the spirit of Amelia,
Wrapped in kelp against the breezing cold;
Silent with a voice so loud,
And nothing in reply is told.
Is she below the saline shore?
In company with the sweet Lenore,
And the much loved Annabelle Lee
In some kingdom by the sea?

Yet it might be just a thought,
Wild in my imaginations fraught,
Dreams of adventures never sought,
Or battles where on "Flanders Field" my favoured comrades fought.
And their loss 'twas all for naught.

This shadowy vestige of a sailing past,
Shapened by myriad winds and waves,
Rests in my hand at last,
Subject to whatever whim my mind,
In its wanderings craves.
And that will henceforth be her lore.
And more I guess we'll never know.
Thank you Edgar Allen Poe.

MY TWO SENSE

Candy Ann was the name of the helicopter that pulled
me from the damp Laotian Jungle on December, 21, 1968,
after I'd been shot down during the unfortunate Vietnam
War. My thoughts often wander back to Tchepone.

THE GRACIELLA EXPERIENCE

Pony Ault was the most socially connected woman in Santa Fe, and my best New Mexico client. It seemed like she knew everyone, and it was not unusual for her to bring celebrities into my gallery to meet me. I loved that about her, and the fact that she could write a check for nearly anything she wanted did not go undetected by my banker and me.

Everyone loved Pony, especially me. She was a chatterbox conversationalist so I always gravitated to her at parties, dinners, and art openings. She took chitchatting to an intellectual plateau that was several layers above where I normally felt at ease. My time with her was usually spent listening, smiling, and nodding. Being seen with her always gave me an ego boost.

Pony told me she wanted a painting by Robert Henri (1865-1929). His paintings were very important and quite valuable, so my eyes were always on alert for his name in auction catalogs.

The problem for me was that Pony had a great eye for art, and this was a trait that worked to my disadvantage. In fact, she sometimes knew more about the artists whose work was hanging on my walls than I did. So when we talked price, I was disarmed and would usually

Robert Henri

capitulate to what she delicately described as her "medicinal discount."

After a few weeks of searching, a Henri painting turned up and I bought it. It was a portrait of a girl named Graciella. When it arrived, for some reason it didn't appeal to me. Her face was, well… I don't know what to say.

So I hung Graciella in my office on the wall opposite my desk, and there she sat for nearly a month while I tried to warm up to her. Every time I looked up, there she was, her stern face staring down at me. Although I didn't ever expect to like her, I did hope that we could at least establish some kind of meaningful rapport.

When I finally called Pony to let her know I had what she was looking for, she made an appointment to see me the next afternoon. She said that she'd be bringing Cary Grant with her. I couldn't have been more excited because *To Catch a Thief* was one of my favorite movies.

The next day when they entered my office, introductions were made and I shook hands with the debonair Mr. Grant. We talked for several minutes and then Pony turned around to face the wall.

There it was in grand lighting, the *Graciella Henri*. She immediately recognized the artist's style, palette, subject, and personality… but she wasn't at all impressed. As if possessed by the spirit of Thor, she turned back around to face me. "Is that what you called me down here for, to look at that thang?"

Her face was unsympathetic and a moment of silence ensued. Before I could respond, she pointed her nose back toward the 17th-century Spanish door to my office, and out she strode with Mr. Grant in close follow. Neither one of them even said goodbye.

Gulp! I went to my refrigerator and took a long pull of Worchestershire Sauce to clear my head.

A couple of weeks later, as if nothing had happened, Pony started coming back around. She liked to show off our gallery to her lunching friends and houseguests. I'd often catch her sneaking glances at the You-Know-What hanging opposite the desk in my office, but each visit ended the same way and she left without comment. I didn't care because Graciella and I were becoming friends.

During an evening art opening at our gallery, Pony open the door to my office and sneaked in. She was in there for a minute or more. That's when I started to worry.

A week later she called me on the phone. "Forrest, I want that painting and I'll be there in 30 minutes to get it." My heart sank. "Pony," I lamented. "You didn't say anything and I've grown to love that 'thang.' I've decided to keep it in my own collection." There was a gravid pause in our conversation while Pony absorbed the news. Then a loud sound pounded against my ear drum. "What!?" she thundered. I felt like my tail was under a rocking chair, and Pony was in the seat.

What could I do but capitulate? After all, she was a good friend and a good client, and I sensed that she was about to have an unfortunate physical issue. Not to mention that I needed the money.

An hour later, my wife walked into the office and asked why I was reading my Bible. I didn't mean to be rude, I just didn't want to talk about it. ∣ f

160

Pony was at her best when hosting her own parties. Moving from one person to another, she'd "light candles" to keep conversations going. I loved watching her at work.

PARTYING WITH SUZANNE SOMERS

Last Saturday, my grandson Shiloh rented a plane and flew me to a party at Suzanne Somers' home in Palm Springs. The weather departing Santa Fe was terrible, and for the first 100 miles I pretty much kept my eyes closed and deferred to my pilot to keep me alive. How can you fly under clouds that are kissing the ground? I didn't want to know. We eventually landed safely and picked up our rental car.

Suzanne's house doesn't have an address, so we received email directions and pulled up to a huge green gate and rang the bell. After convincing the security staff that we weren't terrorists, the gate opened and we drove a few winding blocks to a secluded parking area that was surrounded by ten-foot-high oleanders and palo verde trees. It was like a jungle.

Strangely, the pavement ended and we realized there were no roads within 300 feet of the house (all of the building materials were carried up by burros when it was constructed). So the valets put us in a small open-air tram and pushed a button. Two minutes later, we were halfway up a rocky hillside that contained mountain sheep, bobcats, and rattlesnakes. Suzanne doesn't like rattlesnakes.

When we arrived at the top, our greeters were George Hamilton who had made 57 movies, and a lady with an unforgettable face who had lived with Elvis Presley for seven years (sorry, I forgot her name). Shiloh was impressed, but I tried to appear indifferent.

Suzanne welcomed us warmly and introduced us to some of her friends, one of which was a dashing shipping magnate who wore a white hat and a matching white tie. He was a slight, soft-spoken man who owned three 900-foot-long ocean freighters, and had recently stepped down from a job making $100 million a year running an oil

company. Another was a guy who sold one of the three city blocks he owned in downtown Seattle to Google.

Shiloh, who was 30 years younger than anyone else at the party, flirted with Suzanne's divorced daughter, Leslie, and a billionaire widow who had financed many of the civic organizations around Palm Springs.

Outside, in a natural stone amphitheater that abutted the house, a ten-piece orchestra played Cuban music non-stop. The singer moved to the music, and I swear, her body shook in places that I didn't even know existed. She had to take frequent breaks.

At dinner I sat next to Suzanne and she HAD to introduce me to everyone who came up to chat, about a hundred in all. I felt like a dime at a dollar bill convention.

Later, when the candles were burning low, Shiloh took me to our motel. Then he went back to the party and stayed until the candles died of old age. He denied it, but Leslie told me.

At breakfast the next morning, eight of us sat around Suzanne's kitchen table while her husband, Alan Hamel, cooked eggs over-easy

on corn pone cakes, and grits that were decorated with bitelets of bacon. Suzanne served healthy glasses of a severely green liquid that she described as "a blend." It was made of eight different fruits whose names were foreign to me, except for bananas, but I didn't taste those in the mix. I drank it like it was good for me, and I'm sure it was because Suz is a health nut.

I didn't know the man sitting on my right, but when he was introduced as Arnold Kopelson, I said "Oh," and pretended to understand. Suz knew I didn't though, so she whispered that he had produced 29 movies and received an Oscar for *Platoon*. I smiled and sat up straighter in my chair.

At 10:30 a.m., Shiloh and I jumped back in the Cessna and pointed it 060 degrees for Santa Fe. The strong headwind didn't help our progress so we stopped at Sedona for fuel and buffalo burgers with grilled onions and fries.

Back in the plane, we lost an hour in the time change and it got dark quickly. Shiloh couldn't see the flight instruments, but after fumbling with the switches he got the lights working just in time for us to land at Santa Fe airport.

For an aged kid from a small town in Texas, the Palm Springs experience was both ego-shrinking and mind-expanding. It was nice to see how those people lived, but it was even nicer to be back in my recliner again with a little pinon smoke coming from my fireplace. There is no place like home. f

Suzanne has a bathtub about 100 feet up the side of the mountain from her house. It's just up there all by itself amid the rocks and cactus. Shiloh and I couldn't believe it. I guess she likes to look at wild flowers while she bathes. Probably anyone in town can look too, but I don't know.

MY TWO SENSE

SEP

Bye Forrest.
Bye Shiloh.

THE BULLET COMES HOME

169

My first car was a black, 60-horsepower, 1935 Plymouth Tudor sedan. It was not the deluxe model, so it didn't have a sun visor or windshield wiper on the passenger side.

While driving it from Atlanta, Georgia to Temple, Texas, I sat on a thick book and a pillow so I could see over the dash, and reaching the pedals was a stretch. I drove only at night so the police couldn't see I was a young-looking 15-year-old kid.

The 1,200 miles passed slowly at a speed of 45 mph, but it was love at first sight for me. During the day I curled up on the back seat and dreamed about my beautiful Plymouth.

It had no safety glass in the windows, no trunk, no air conditioner or radio, no power steering or power brakes, and no turn signals. But I could lever the windshield up to get ventilation. It was great.

Peggy named my wonderful car "The Bullet," because she said it was shot. Out of respect, we never used that term when we were within earshot of the car.

When we were in high school, in the late 1940s, I'd take Peggy home for lunch, and 30 minutes later, pick her up again. We always had a few minutes to sit in the *Bullet*, listening to Eddy Arnold on the portable radio while waiting for the bell to ring. Gas was 11 cents and I often pulled into a station and bought two gallons for a quarter, saving the three cents change for next time.

When Peggy and I wanted to go out on a date, like for a burger and a movie at the Arcadia

about 1946

170

Theatre, I'd pawn my two-dollar bill with her mom. I was always able to buy it out of hock by babysitting or mowing the neighbor's lawn. I still have that two dollar bill, but it looks a little wallet-worn. I am trying to decide where to leave it when I'm gone. It can't be left just anyplace.

When I went to Yellowstone with my parents in 1950, Peggy drove the *Bullet* for three months while I was away. I really missed both of them.

The following autumn, three eventful things happened: Peggy started school at the University of Houston, I joined the Air Force and went off to basic training, and something mysterious happened to the *Bullet*. When I came home on my first leave, the car had vanished and no one around town was willing to talk about it. I went into mourning and never did get my car back.

Sixty-three years later I offered to give $250 to anyone who could find it. Later, when I mentioned it to my friend Richard Blake, who is a serious car nut and has nine garages at his house, he went to work.

It took some long months for Richard to find the *Bullet's* twin brother. It was in Maryland and it wasn't $250 anymore. With one

about 70 years later

photograph by
Lacee Peloquin

171

email, I came out of mourning. All of a sudden, instead of feeling old, I felt like I'd ripened again.

When the Plymouth arrived, I drove it around town for a couple of months but it wasn't the same. I ran out of gas because when the tank read half-full, it was empty. My 85-year-old arms grew weary trying to turn, and once when it was raining, I got flooded trying to signal a left turn (mainly because I had to hand-crank the crazy window down and stick my arm out). The windshield wiper stopped in the middle of a thunderstorm, and I had to pull over and wait it out.

Besides all of that, Peggy wasn't in the mood to ride in a 65-year-old car. The moment had passed for us, and the ambience was gone. Richard Blake sold the car for me and I lost $4,000 on it. I don't know what happened, but they don't make romance like they used to. f

MY TWO SENSE

There's an old sentiment that says, "Once you leave home you can never move back," and I believe it. The Bullet was important to me at a time in my life when I was gathering speed, so to speak. Now it is only an important memory.

THE PRICE OF FREEDOM

173 History will not say that Alex LaFountain was a great sculptor, unless you throw grit and character into the mix as requirements to that end. Then he would nicely fit the description.

In 1967, I met him at an art show in Great Falls, Montana. His bronzes were spread out on a display in front of us, and we spoke about him casting his work in his own foundry. I was impressed because I was just teaching myself the craft of lost wax casting in my own garage back in Lubbock. He shared some ideas with me that were helpful.

As I turned to leave, Alex reached into a box and pulled out something that gave me pause. It was an original wax model of a wolf. I thought it was wonderful, and he handed it to me. The poor animal, with hair standing up on his back and ribs hard-pressing against his skin, was chewing his leg off to gain independence from a steel trap. His turned up muzzle showed snarling contempt for whoever laid that horrible device in his wait.

I purchased the model from Alex with the handshake understanding that it would cast in only 30 copies.

I quickly made the mold and started casting bronzes. The first one I poured was #28 because I wanted to work the casting bugs out before making the lower numbers, which would be more valuable. I named it *The Price of Freedom*. Twenty-eight of the copies were sold over time, but I liked #28 so much I've kept it all of these years. I also kept the #1 copy, but I can't remember why.

Something Alex taught me is that valor can lay hidden in the human spirit for many years, with no requirement to expose its existence. Then, with only a moment's notice, it can reveal itself in astonishing ways. That's how heroes are made.

In 1971, Alex and his wife were floating down the Missouri River on a sunny afternoon near Great Falls. He heard a frantic voice crying out, and noticed a friend floundering in the water. Alex dove in and swam to the rescue. His friend was saved, but Alex was pulled under and disappeared in the sweep of water.

Every time I look at *The Price of Freedom* I think of Alex, and how tentative life is for all of God's creatures. f

174

MY TWO SENSE

Casting art bronze was a dangerous business for me because I had to teach myself how to do it. My first hard-way lesson came as I poured 2,100 degree metal from the crucible into a mold. There was spillage, and moisture in my concrete driveway quickly turned to steam and blew up in my face. The plastic visor saved my eyes, and that's when the angels told me to pour over sand.

TIME

The Weekly Newsmagazine

Volume XXV   JEROME HERMAN DEAN   Number 15

ME AND DIZZY DEAN

In 1955 I was at the Texas Open golf tournament in San Antonio walking on my way to someplace when I heard a booming voice "Hey kid they got any cold beer around here?" I stopped and looked about. There were lots of people milling but none of them were paying attention to me so I thought it must be an aberration.

"Hey feller I'm up here" the voice bellowed. I was standing beside a ladder that climbed straight up about 10 feet to a platform where I saw an arm wildly waving at me. "Think you could find a couple of cold ones somewhere?"

The arm belonged to Dizzy Dean and I recognized his beaming face right off. He played for several teams including the St. Louis Cardinals and was the last pitcher in the National League to win 30 games in one season.

He was one of my all-time favorite baseball heroes (along with the ageless Satchel Paige who famously said "How old would I be if I didn't know how old I wuz?"

About 10 minutes later I climbed the ladder holding a six pack of Jax beer and a Dr. Pepper. My cost was almost 2 bucks but I didn't care

because this was *Dizzy Dean*. I was thrilled even more than when I shook hands with Sammy Baugh. Dizzy was commentating on the radio between sips and talking with me during commercials and more sips.

It was Sunday afternoon and as the tournament wound down Dizzy finished off the last Jax and my bottle of soda was almost done. We said our good-byes and I climbed down the ladder expecting to see a bunch of photographers recording me and Dizzy. There weren't any but it was an experience I've enjoyed for the last 63 years. | **f**

179

I've been criticized for the way I write and use words. I say I too much, mix verb tenses, use commas wrong, and I can't spell. I just read through my story above about Dizzy Dean, and removed all of the commas. I feel so good I may just go get myself another Dr. Pepper.

COLOPHON

Ω

ONCE UPON A WHILE *revised*

2017

CREATIVE DIRECTOR
Bruno Advertising + Design, *Santa Fe, New Mexico*

DESIGN & PRODUCTION
S Caldwell Design, *Santa Fe, New Mexico*

BODY TEXT
Adobe Garamond

TITLE TEXT
Executive

PAPER STOCK
Platinum Silk 100lb. text

PRINTED & BOUND BY
Starline Printing, *Albuquerque, New Mexico*

ILLUSTRATIONS BY
Dreamstime.com : (background art) cover and pages 164-165 ©Elena Schweitzer,
©Flas100 – pages ii-iii, ©Anna Rudenko page iv-v, ©Anikasalera pages 66, 69,
©Rudchenkol pages 66, 69, ©Arfo pages 58-59, ©Natalie Khlapushyna page 141,
and ©R.Gino Santa Maria page 156